Yorkie Doodle Dandy

Or, The Other Woman Was A Real Dog

Yorkie Doodle Dandy
by William A. Wynne

© 2017 Smoky War Dog LLC
© 1996 William A. Wynne

Seventh Printing 2017

Library of Congress Catalog Card Number: 96-90158

ISBN 0-9652254-0-3

Published by: Smoky War Dog LLC
Hinckley, Ohio
http://smokywardog.com

Cover art and photographic layout:
Donald Esmond
Cleveland, Ohio

North Coast Litho, Inc.
Cleveland, Ohio

Book Layout:
Marcia Wynne Deering
St. Louis, Missouri

To Margie

YORKIE DOODLE DANDY

A MEMOIR

BY WILLIAM A. WYNNE

TABLE OF CONTENTS

Introduction

YORKIE DOODLE DANDY

In the context of the greatest devastation in planet Earth's history, and the subsequent eradication of over 100 million human beings peopling it, the story about a dog in World War II is indeed insignificant.

But wars, large or small, are made up of millions of stories experienced by those involved in the war itself or by those remaining at home. From the broad point of view of nations being pulverized or vaporized, any personal experience is less than a footnote. Yet, for individuals who are thrust into such catastrophes, a time comes when little things become big things.

This was brought out in 1990, during a late-night television news broadcast of an interview with an American soldier in the Kuwait desert. The soldier said of the lengthening waiting; the days, weeks, months: "We began to appreciate small things as we never did before." Someone received a yo-yo. He and his companions became delighted just making it go up and down.

Smoky's and my war story is about a little thing that became bigger after the war.

Our postwar story is perhaps a bit more tangible. We continued in the entertainment field and pioneered in television. Raising a growing family in the era of "baby boomers" to make ends meet, there was always the "real job." The real jobs were necessary because being home with Margie and the children was most important. My being from a broken family was enough for me to resolve it would never happen in my family.

No doubt working as a flight photographer in Icing Research for NACA/NASA would be more than exciting employment for most people, without being on stage. Also working as a photojournalist for one of the largest newspapers is hardly dull work. The newspaper work came for the most part, later.

This story though is mostly about a mighty little dog I was fortunate enough to have. A dog that was shared with millions of others. In 1995, William Hennessee of Sherman Grinberg Library—N.Y. Commercial archivist of Paramount 1927-57/ABC News, after viewing Smoky in the 1946 Newsreel taken at Great Lakes Naval Base Hospital in Illinois, commented "it was funny." In peace time after 50 years Smoky was still funny. You might imagine how much fun she was under the stresses of war. Fun and humor was the point of her whole existence. And now some are saying Smoky is the greatest dog of all.

No one accomplishes anything alone in this world and credit is due to many. I want to thank my wife, Margie and my mother, Beatrice Caffrey Wynne, for the typing, correcting and editing they both provided immediately after World War II; permitting the assembling of stories which formed the base on which large parts of this book are constructed. It is amazing how much of that sort of information the mind forgets over many years. Their earlier work has been invaluable.

Thanks to Martin T. Ranta, a retired editor of the Cleveland PLAIN DEALER, who generously took on the task of editing this book, stealing time from his family on top of working as a copy editor with the San Diego Union and Marty's wife, Virginia, who assisted. To my daughter, Marcia Wynne Deering, of Ballwin, Missouri, for typing edited copy and helping in research and publishing. To Max Riddle, the ultimate dog expert, who graciously wrote in the FOREWORD what he has been telling people for years. To the Richland County, Ohio Madison Branch librarians, who searched for and borrowed books for reference from all over the State of Ohio.

Thanks to the friends from the 26th Photo Squadron: former Commanding Officer, Dr. George B. Gathers, Jr., Bill Bishop, John Brown, Irv Green and others for their contributions. To Suzanne Hively, Dog Columnist for the PLAIN DEALER, and Sports Writer, Len Haas who both encouraged me in difficult times to continue working on this book. And Don Esmond who made prints, photocopies, did research, made and changed layouts, maps and book assembly and who from the beginning of our joining the 26th Photo, is still a faithful friend.

YORKIE DOODLE DANDY

FOREWORD

In very ancient times, dogs accompanied invading armies. But, for the most part, they were used to round up game from the countryside, and thus, partly for sport. If dogs were savage they might, in the excitement of battle, attack their own soldiers. Probably, most of the true war dogs were used as armor bearers. Many wore light mail, including spiked collars.

From the Battle of Agincourt on October 25, 1514, one name stands out, that of Sir Peers Legh of Lyme Hall in England. He had taken his favorite Mastiff bitch with him. Sir Peers was wounded, but his dog guarded him until the next day, when he returned to Paris. He died there and his body and dog were returned to Lyme Hall. The bitch became the founding member of one of the most famous lines of English Mastiffs.

The first World War found dogs doing a variety of services. Some helped to string telephone wires. Some did messenger service, or Red Cross rescue work. Still others guarded prisoners, and alerted troops in trenches. Alaskan sled dogs worked in the mountains.

Two dogs, both German Shepherds, became world famous as motion picture actors. One was Rin Tin Tin. He had been left as a puppy in a dugout at Metz during a German retreat. He was acquired by Lieutenant Lee Duncan, an American, who nursed the puppy to a healthy adulthood, took him back to California, and gave him superior training. The dog became world famous as a canine actor. Although he was unregistered, half a dozen Rin Tin Tin's have kept his name and fame alive.

Another captured German Shepherd was registered. His name was Strongheart. A brother to Strongheart was imported and placed at stud. Although he sired hundreds of puppies, they proved to be of very poor quality, both mentally and physically. His offspring did great harm to the reputation of the breed, perhaps because so many got into the wrong hands.

And now we come to a third, this one a product of World War II. Rin Tin Tin was lucky to fall into the hands of an experienced trainer of German Shepherd dogs. This third dog was as lucky as Rin Tin Tin had been. And her origin is even a greater mystery. Her trainer had still to mature. So dog and trainer grew together. That dog became a miracle—the greatest dog I ever knew, and far greater than any I have read about.

So now, read about Bill Wynne and his truly miraculous Yorkshire Terrier, Smoky.

Maxwell Riddle*

*Maxwell Riddle, the man in the tuxedo seen judging dog shows at the CRUFT'S in London, WESTMINSTER in N.Y., Paris, Tokyo, Sydney or South America is considered the foremost living authority on dogs. When not judging, for almost 70 years Riddle has covered the major dog shows, field and tracking trials, motion picture dogs and personally raised 53 breeds to learn more about dogs. A syndicated columnist, author or co-author of 14 dog specialty books, a contributor to regular and dog encyclopedias, Riddle is associate editor of DOG WORLD MAGAZINE and winner of The National Book Award in 1987 for his book DOGS THROUGH HISTORY. The DOG WRITERS of AMERICA named its MAXWELL AWARDS in honor of Max Riddle. The awards are given annually for the best dog column and video.

PART ONE

CHAPTER 1

A NEW FOUND FRIEND

It was George Washington's birthday, 1957. The family, bundled against February's cold, drove to the Metropark on Cleveland's west side. We were a somber group, marching slowly, single-file down Riverside Drive to our destination. I carried a shovel, a pick, and, under my arm, a shoe box. We were on a burial detail.

More than thirteen years had passed since that day in early March 1944 when Smoky and I met in Nadzab, New Guinea. The war with Japan was in full force and we were at the base closest to the front.

The first time I saw her was in a darkened tent at the 5212th Photographic Wing motor pool. She was an unbelievable mite of a thing, spinning like a whirling dervish, jumping and bumping my legs. I bent down until we were face to face. "What kind of beast is this?" I asked myself. I was looking into a grinning fuzzy face. Almond eyes laughed at me above a jet, black, button nose, and a friendly pink tongue licked my hand. A closer examination revealed this creature to be a female dog with gold-colored head and legs and a gray-blue body. Her stubby tail wagged in a blur. Her size was unreal! She was no taller than my GI shoes and not much longer.

She was tied to a huge truck tire by a white parachute shroud. A makeshift collar was wrapped around her neck, which was no bigger than a woman's wrist. Her hair was coarsely chopped as though it had been done by a sickle. Her head was the size of a baseball, her ears resembled miniature windmill blades, and her weight was almost nothing at all.

Setting the dog down and heading back to the parked vehicles. I found Sergeant Dare bending under the hood of a jeep trying to adjust the ignition. He heard me approach and looked back over his shoulder from under his pith helmet. "What do you think it is?" he asked.

"A dizzy little poodle of some sort." I replied. "Hey, Dare. I'll give you two pounds Australian for her."

"Make it three and she's yours," he answered.

I wasn't sure she would live. She seemed so weak. I told him that.

Dare explained how Ed Downey, my buddy from Norristown, Pennsylvania, had found the mutt. He was driving a jeep on one of the many primitive roads around the Wing area, snaking through kunai grass and the jungle, when the jeep suddenly quit. Downey climbed out, lifted the hood and started jiggling the wires. He heard whimpering by the side of the road. Walking toward the sound, he saw a furry blonde head bobbing up and then disappearing. Moving closer, he discovered a tiny dog trying to climb out of an abandoned foxhole. Downey, an avowed dog hater, grabbed the pup, tossed it on the seat of the jeep and went back to pushing the wires onto the spark plugs. When the engine kicked over, he returned to the motor pool. Showing Dare what he had found, he offered it to him. Dare called the dog, Smokums.

Dare immediately chopped off the dog's hair. " The mutt was too hot," he said. Chopped was the word for it, all right. Next, he cut a shroud from a parachute and attached it to a collar he had fashioned from a narrow belt.

Arriving back at our tent, I asked Ed. "How come you didn't offer me the dog? You know I've been wanting to get one."

"I don't want a mutt in my tent," he stated flatly. We let the matter drop.

The next day. I was working in the photo trailer under Captain Powell, who was involved in photographic equipment development, when Dare came knocking at the door.

"Hey, Wynne, do you want to buy the dog for the two pounds? I want to get back in a poker game tonight," he declared, laughing, his trim mustache twitching under his helmet.

"How is she looking today?" I asked suspiciously.

"Great! All she needed was a couple of good meals," he assured me.

The deal was made. Two pounds Australian were transferred.

The American equivalent of each pound was $3.22. That $6.44 was about ten percent of a PFC's monthly pay, including overseas pay. I was willing to meet the price.

I could hardly wait until quitting time to claim that weird little creature for my own and give some serious attention to her physical condition.

What a greeting I got! She was twice as enthusiastic as the day before. Dare was right, she was feeling much better. With my thumb and forefinger encircling her back near her hips. I could tell that she was slightly bony, perhaps, but not too bad. Her teeth were second teeth, but sharp. Her eyes were clear, her ears stood up well, and that stubby tail was docked just after the first joint. Her greatest asset, though, was her spirit! She was a rollicking bundle of fuzz and energy as we made our way back to our tent. Downey was on his cot. He looked up and yelled, "I don't want a mutt in my tent!"

I stated calmly. "She's staying."

After a long moment of silence, he said, "Well, keep it away from me."

The South West Pacific Area (SWPA) where we were stationed was a less important battle ground at the time than the European Theater of Operation (ETO). Part of the Allied mission was to hold off the Japanese advance to Australia and attempt to regain Asia, thus forcing an eventual Japanese surrender. It was not expected, though, that we could do this without help from our forces fighting in Europe. That help was supposed to come after Hitler's defeat. We were making some progress but our numbers and our supplies were limited.

Ed Downey and I were aerial photographers who came overseas as casuals, not permanently assigned to a specific unit but acting as replacements in squadrons already in the Pacific. Our first assignment was with the 5th Fighter Command of the 5th Air Force at Port Moresby, New Guinea. Downey was a bit of a swashbuckler, an Errol Flynn type. He was a tall, cocky, athletic redhead with a great sense of humor. Our first home in the sweltering heat of Port Moresby was a pyramid-shaped tent on a hill overlooking the jungle on one side and the airfield on the other. The tent's location made the most of a balmy breeze which the Regular Army veterans of the tropics knew would minimize the mosquito hazard.

Inside our canvas home we found World War I helmets and some ugly old bug-eyed gas masks. It was December 1943 and most of the men who had survived earlier campaigns had gone home, leaving this outdated equipment behind. Others were preparing to leave as replacements were coming in.

We adapted quickly to our surroundings. Every day several red alerts warned us to take cover. At night, searchlights swept the sky, occasionally framing a high-altitude "washing machine Charlie" in the lights, and the anti-aircraft (ack-ack) guns blasted away. Sometimes as many as ten bombers at one time came in and plastered our airstrips. This was far fewer than the 150 planes hitting the area six months before.

After several weeks of simple work details, Downey and I complained to the Inspector General that we were aerial photographers, not general soldiers. Soon we were transferred. We were attached to the 5212th

3

Photo Wing under General David W. Hutchinson (Photo Hutch) and sent to Nadzab, New Guinea. (Another general, Donald Hutchinson was nicknamed Fighter Hutch.) We were supposed to be Photo Hutch's personal aerial photographers, but when we arrived we learned that he was in the hospital. On December 26, 1943, a B-17 loaded with photographers, newsreel men and Hutch had crashed on a mission to cover the invasion of Cape Glouster, New Britain.

And that's why we were where we were.

Having faced down Ed and his objection to having a dog in his tent, my next concern was finding food for my diminutive canine companion. I wondered whether I could feed a dog in the tropics on Army rations. Our chow consisted of coffee, dehydrated potatoes, powdered milk and eggs, bully beef (a kind of canned hash we got from the Aussies), mutton (awful in odor and taste) and citric acid to drink. The latter was to prevent scurvy. Happily, canned fruit was plentiful and fruit cocktail was our favorite. Less popular was the canned tropical butter, always soft but never quite able to melt on your food or, more annoyingly, in your mouth. I fed my Smoky a half canteen cup of bully beef.

The name Smoky seemed appropriate because of her coloring. It was a smooth, easy name for calls and recalls. I had already decided to train her to obedience trials and tricks. Time was no problem. There was little to do in our spare time but write letters home or watch movies at night. Of course, this was between running back and forth to our foxholes during the nuisance air raids by the enemy. At first they were day and night, then later, nights only as the Allies slowly gained air superiority. Smoky was seven inches tall at the shoulder and weighed only four pounds, so I didn't think it would be too difficult to keep her, even in a war zone.

Her training began simply enough. Using the parachute shroud and her little collar, I began her first lessons in obedience. It was, "Heel!" "Sit!" "Heel!" "Stand stay!" At this last command she was expected to stay where she was, not moving, while I walked away and then walked back. I was teaching her to obey my firm commands, but I was also encouraging her with lots of play and praise. I was determined not to overdo the training. Smoky took to it all very quickly. She was game for the work and loved taking breaks for walks or playing tug-of-war with a sock. And it was enjoyable for me too. I felt like a kid again!

An editor advised it was important that information about the author be placed near the front in a story like this, please bear with me. As Margie says, "get out the violins, Bill is going to start when he was five years old." Much of the following monologue is given in lectures on creative photography (my real life) because it delves into sensitivity in observation powers through living experience and this applies to all arts using the science of experimentation.

Remember this. A dog is only as good as his trainer-handler. In Hollywood it is said, "a great dog and poor handler will go nowhere. A fair dog and great handler will get by, but with a great handler and great dog—the sky's the limit." This may be said of all athletes be they human or animal in any competition or performance. The greatness of both consists of natural ability, with desire to over achieve, will to win, and the confidence to rely on each other has to be in both the coach and athlete. For the human or animal trainer, part of the personal make-up is the extreme desire to win, be the best and nothing short will do. Football coaches call it intestinal fortitude, or willingness to pay the price.

Your background is part of what you are, the way you see, think and execute. Now all through my hectic childhood, the refuge in companionship of pets was part of my development. For photojournalism however all life experience affects why we see the way we do, which direction we choose to aim the camera and why we select that particular moment to press the shutter button, a much more complex treatise.

I was born in Scranton, Pennsylvania, on March 29, 1922. My parents lived in Cleveland, Ohio, but my mother wanted to be with her mother in Scranton when I was born. Two weeks later I was on the train back to Cleveland, my permanent home.

My parents, Martin Wynne and Beatrice Caffrey Wynne, were both born in Scranton. Grandpa Caffrey, a coal miner, died suddenly at the age of 40. Mother, the eldest of eight children, left school at 15 to help support the family. Her brother, Jack, stayed in school until the sixth grade and then left to become a broker boy in the anthracite mines. It was not uncommon in those days for children to sacrifice their educations to help their families financially. Jack, with his elementary education, built a tiny suburban Chicago office into the John Hancock Insurance Company's largest office in volume business with 59 agents in the 1950s. Mother completed two years of higher education, earning the Kappa Kappa Phi Honor Key (KKP). Phi Beta Kappa and KKP later merged and now Cleveland College she attended is part of Case Western Reserve University.

By the time I was six, mother was an office manager supervising forty women at the Smith Standard Co., a manufacturer of Chick Incubators.

My parents had split up in 1925 and I never saw my dad or heard from him or received any money from him after that. The Irish name Keegan and Irish-welsh Wynne of Pennsylvania were grandparents on that side.

Mother was working full time and finding it impossible to get competent child care for me and my younger brother, Jim. So, we were temporarily placed in Parmadale orphanage in Parma, Ohio. This institution was operated by the Catholic Diocese of Cleveland. I was there for two years, Jim for one. My older sister, Mary, lived with our grandmother in Scranton.

Early on, her well-paying position at the incubator company made it a bit easier. We even had a live-in housekeeper for two years. Mother's wonderful job evaporated in the middle of the Depression, as was the case for so many other working people. Her next position, one of great responsibility but far less pay, supported her for the rest of her working days. A woman's salary, even if she was the main support of her family, was always less than a man's wages.

At Parmadale, I lived in a pleasant English-style cottage, Number 13, with 39 other boys under the guidance of one overworked nun of the Sisters of Charity of St. Augustine. I was very lonely because of the separation from my family and took an early interest in animals as companions. First Sister Lucy and then Sister Hubert were flustered because of the wild animals the boys brought home. We entertained turtles, big black racer snakes, raccoons and, once, two owls from the forest behind our cottage. Two of our boys had gently wrapped the owls in their sweaters and plucked them from their low-limbed perch. The owls hooted all night, prompting an owl-release order from Sister Hubert.

The first of many dogs in my life was Rags, a big, shaggy, wire-haired Airedale. He loved kids and most of us loved him, and we romped the grounds at Parmadale together. One day a surly eighth grader took his anger out on the poor dog by throwing acid at him. Rags was badly burned and the memory of his running in panic and yelping in pain will be with me forever.

A main lesson in life I learned involved baseball. All the boys were gathered into teams with the six year old boys added to those under 10. Selected team leaders picked in rotation choosing those with known athletic prowess or friends until all the teams were filled. That left a miserable looking tribe of castoffs with just enough for the director to make us into another team. We were a spirited bunch learning the game

6

quickly and at the end of the season we won the championship. No dads or moms to cheer us on, fight for us. With little bickering it was straight and pure baseball. That lesson proved there is always hope, anything can be accomplished. Important in this story.

When I came home from Parmadale, I found a large white collie tied to a door knob in the kitchen. This was Skippy. During the few years that we had him, I remember that he was always tied to something. If he got loose, it took all the kids in the neighborhood to catch him because he ran back and forth between us like a fullback daring the defensive line to tackle him. One night Skippy wakened the family next door with his loud barking, something they didn't appreciate. When they discovered their house was on fire, they realized that Skippy had saved their lives. He was a hero.

Our home was always filled with people. During the depression, families crowded in together, sharing whatever housing was available. My grandmother, Bridget Durkin Caffrey, "Mom" from Scranton, Uncle Jack Caffrey and his wife, Mildred, Aunts Lucille and Helene and Uncle Bill all lived with us. Aunt Pauline came earlier and married Charlie Adler. We were a magnificent family, giving strength to each other during these hard times. In time, each founded separate households, but all remained close-knit for the rest of their lives. At the age of eight, I was quite suddenly introduced to another wonderful dog and to my first human best friend. One sunny summer day, I was startled by a great commotion of shouting and barking and the sound of steel wheels screeching across brick pavement on W. 119th Street.

First to catch my eye were two big boys on bikes wheeling around a kid my age on roller skates who was hanging on to a huge brindle Great Dane. The dog was running in full stride, while his master, in tow, was swaying like a runaway chariot. As the massive dog pulled the skater from curb to curb, the brothers on bikes constantly herded the pair toward the center of the road. In no time at all, the group was upon me, and the huge canine had knocked me down and pinned me to the ground. As the friendly monster slurped my face with his tongue, his tow-ee, Georgie Harsa, tripped on the tree lawn and tumbled on top of us.

Georgie and his dog, Big Boy, and I became instant friends. George's family lived in an apartment over their family bakery on Lorain Avenue near W. 118th Street. Big Boy stood seven feet on his hind legs, and when he ran through the apartment, the floors shook and his whip-like tail sent chairs scattering in every direction.

Once in a while I helped George wash and dry the big cookie sheets at the bakery. My reward was always a bag of delicious lady fingers and mouth-watering custard puffs. That was in 1931 when, for many people, just getting enough to eat was an accomplishment. I have never been paid so well!

I loved to sit and listen to George practicing his banjo and singing his 'Beginner Classic' song, "Oh bury me not on the lone prairie, where the coyotes howl and the wind blows free." I lost my fun-loving friend, George Harsa, in May 1943 when his B-17 bomber crashed on a Texas prairie during a training flight. He was brought home to Cleveland for burial.

I was an introverted child. Because of the enforced discipline required to control the large number of children at Parmadale, many of us withdrew into ourselves. Punishment was administered by slaps on the hand with a two-inch wide, half-inch thick wooden stick. A child was expected to hold out his hand for the smacks and was more severely punished if he pulled his hand away.

All in all, pleasant memories from Parmadale outnumber unpleasant ones. My first grade teacher, Sister Rose Frances, told my wife years later that I was a good student. Those days ended abruptly when I was slammed into Cleveland City Hospital with scarlet fever a few days after Christmas. In the ensuing months, the patients in the contagious ward gave me chicken pox, mumps and measles. In those days, the health department came to private homes to post a red quarantine sign on the door to warn others of these diseases. There was no such protection for me in the hospital. I was still there watching sky rockets outside my window on July Fourth.

I went back to Parmadale briefly and returned home just in time for second grade. Yet observation has always been one of my best teachers. It helped me to understand a great deal about dogs. I know what kind of family lives in a house by observing its dog. If the dog is calm, slow-paced, his people are quiet and serene. A charging, excitable dog probably lives with children. When I was a boy, neighborhood dogs ran free and became friends with people according to their moods. One day you might be received as an old and welcome friend and on another occasion be completely ignored by the same animal.

Queenie was a nondescript stray who "followed me home" and mother let me keep her. She had a litter of six pups before she was killed in traffic. Pal, one of her pups, was a mix of Chow- Brindle Bull, Staffordshire Terrier and a number of unspecified breeds, a magnificent beast of pure muscle. I gave him to a buddy and we shared him thereafter. Pal loved all humankind and was very gentle in our company, but he was a terror with other male dogs. His diet, mostly table scraps, left his teeth in poor condition, decayed and broken. Because he was part Bulldog, he loved to fight and took on dogs much larger than himself. Fortunately for them, his poor teeth kept him from inflicting much damage. Pal was an eager pupil. He was willing to ride downhill, precariously balanced on a sled, and then drag all our piled-up sleds back up the hill just because I told him to do it. He would, on command, leap six feet into the air and snatch a knitted cap from my head, shake it and then drop it when I yelled, "Stop!"

When our gang went swimming, we had to cross some heavily traveled streets. "Up!" sent Pal flying into my arms so that I could carry him safely across. I also used this command to keep him under control when I spotted a rival dog before he did. Pal figured out, on his own, where my school was and met me there every day at 3:30 to share the mile walk home. One afternoon, he wasn't there. He wasn't at home, either. For months I waited for him, but I never saw him again. It broke my heart.

Most of my school years were disastrous. Because of the Depression, we moved around a lot, looking for better housing one year, cheaper housing the next, according to our economic status.

As a result, I attended three different elementary schools and moved ten times before I was 17. My in-school hours were spent staring out the windows, dreaming, waiting for school to be out and for my real day to begin with Pal outdoors in the fields.

The city was sprawling and fascinating for young boys. In the spring we looked for mudpuppies in a large rain pond behind the Sears store. Sometimes we played at the sand field, a large vacant lot covering an area ten city blocks long and four city blocks deep at Triskett Road on the West-Side. The sand field had what we called Indian mounds, low abrupt hills calling for skillful bike riding. There was a ball field and a high billboard backed by struts for climbing. Nearby were scrub woods filled with songbirds, including bob-o-links, and a swamp that was frequented by a variety of water birds. These were wonderful places for Pal and me to explore.

During the day, we played endless games of football, baseball and street hockey. Our puck was a crushed tin can and our sticks were leftovers from brooms. On summer nights, we played kick-the-can, relieval, horse and hunchy-go-punchy. Sometimes I passed the time riding the bike I had bought for a buck.

Although my school performance was disappointing, the presence of my large family, good friends and all our dogs, along with the freedom to roam the city, made life a pleasant one. There was very little money, but I can say enthusiastically that my childhood was a great one and I would not trade it for any other.

In the seventh grade, I was invited to play night football on a team sponsored by Frank's Grill. We were a 105-pound average league with an upper age limit of 16. A family friend, Jake Leicht, who later directed the yearly Knights of Columbus track meets in Cleveland had arranged for me to join the team to get me off the streets.

In high school my study efforts improved considerably. West Technical High School was the second largest public school in the country with an enrollment of 5,600 students, bigger than many small colleges. Among many famous alumni are comedian Kay Ballard and President Clinton cabinet member, Donna Shalala, Secretary of Health and Human Services. Its curriculum offered every imaginable subject and its faculty was top-notch. Among the technical courses were machine shop, aircraft engine repair, foundry, pattern making, print shop, carpentry shop, electrical shop, photography and art (I studied photography for one year).

All courses were geared to serve the industries in Ohio. The school also offered complete college prep and business courses. In line with my interest in nature, I studied horticulture in the world's largest high school greenhouse. Before World War II, northern Ohio had more acreage under glass than the rest of the world combined. In three years, our outstanding teacher, Albert T. Haag, taught us the Cornell University horticulture course.

I loved football. West Tech had huge football teams, both in numbers and in size. After two years on the scrubs, I had a brief career on the first team. Before the season started, torn ligaments in the right knee ended my senior year football hopes. During the junior year, we had moved to Joan Avenue near tree-shaded West Boulevard. There life took a happy turn. Margie Roberts lived down the street on Joan Avenue and we became sweethearts.

For my 20th birthday in 1942, Margie gave me a six-week-old puppy that was a mix of German Shepherd and Doberman Pinscher. When the pup, Toby, was six months old, the Cleveland All Breed Training School began giving classes in obedience training for amateurs as part of an effort to supply dogs for the war. It was a national movement sanctioned by the American Kennel Club, and many fine military dogs were trained in this way. Through this program I got the only formal dog training lessons I ever had. These obedience classes were held on Cleveland's downtown public square, where they drew lots of attention and brought more people and dogs into the program.

I had been working part time for Cleveland's largest florist and was offered a full time position there, but the high pay of defense work drew me away. I found employment at the American Steel and Wire Works where I labored near a 1,500 degree furnace annealing high carbon steel. Because there wasn't time to take Toby home after classes and still get to work on time, permission was granted to bring him to the job. During my shift, the dog slept quietly on the warm bricks.

I was half way through the ten-week obedience course, under Mrs. Dewey Satterfield, when I was drafted. The steel works offered me a deferment. The work was brutal. We put in seven days a week, sometimes working two shifts a day. Lead poisoning was the biggest hazard. A forced laxative at the dispensary was guided by the safety dept. With these things in mind, I turned down the deferment:

"No, thanks! I'll take my chances with the WAR!"

Now I was in far-off New Guinea trying to train this little dog with a leather collar instead of the regular choke collar we had used in Cleveland. Smoky learned very fast, picking up my communications with ease. Getting your thoughts into the head of an animal is like teaching a toddler. You must literally show the dog what to do, lead it through the procedure and then encourage and reward it with lots of praise. She had a great eagerness to please.

During the first few days of training Smoky learned to play dead and to sing. The singing part caused some difficulty with one of our tent buddies. He insisted, "When a dog cries, someone is going to die." He was most serious about it, so we were careful to practice that trick only when he was away. The trick started with my playing the harmonica and then switching to prompt her with my voice, "OWOOOOOOOOOO."

Smoky became a tremendous morale booster. I had much to do in the military but she gave me an escape from the loneliness of the New Guinea jungle. Once again, a dog had come to my rescue.

I had been assigned to the photo lab under Captain Powell, whose photo-research unit was organized after he developed a simple aerial-camera mount for low level bombing photography. Unexpectedly, we received transfer orders. Downey went to the 20th Combat Mapping Squadron and I was ordered to the 26th Photo Reconnaissance Squadron.

The 26th Photo was a close-knit squadron formed in 1943. The executive officer was Captain Hartwell McCullough from Louisiana, and the first sergeant was Joyce B. Howell (J.B.), a stocky, fortyish, jet-black-haired Texan. They had been among the first men cut into the squadron, and they remained the heart and soul of this top-notch squadron throughout the war in the Far Pacific.

My high school photography course had opened the door to AAF Photo School at Lowery Field in Colorado, where a lab Tech course was completed in June, 1943. I was then classified as an aerial photographer, having completed another course at Peterson Field near Colorado Springs. They were unsure where to place me—in camera repair, where I could do installations of aerial cameras in P-38s, or in a photo lab.

It was decided that the photo lab was most in need of manpower.

My assignment did not involve flying because the squadron planes were the one-seat fighter type, holding only a pilot. The Lockheed Lightning P-38 (P for pursuit) was a non-traditional plane with a gracefully slim silhouette in flight and twin tail booms supporting whistling superchargers that gave it its unique sound. The photo reconnaissance versions of the P-38 were called F-5s. The young pilots flew alone over targets without guns or fighter protection. Their mission was to get in, get pictures and get out. It has been said that the side with the best photo reconnaissance wins the war. Squadrons like ours were at or near the front at all times. You had a great time watching photo-recon on TV in the Gulf War.

Our group was going full-tilt at this point with two 12-hour shifts a day in the photo lab. Pilots were flying continuous missions. We were not all spit and polish and regulation, though. The Texas flag flew over the orderly room every day and First Sergeant Howell sported cowboy boots instead of GI boots. The outfit had a non-regulation still which I had mistaken for a GI laundry when I stumbled over the large, steaming drums deep in the jungle. Two shorts-clad, sweat-soaked GIs were usually in attendance.

Officially, we stocked a thirty-day supply of food, gasoline for our land vehicles, aviation fuel, medical supplies, photographic film, printing paper and photographic chemicals plus whatever else was needed to keep the squadron operating if isolated.

The next military objective in the war was Hollandia. Commander Lieutenant General Adachi of the Japanese 18th army had declared Hollandia, in Dutch New Guinea, to be the base he would withdraw to with his troops to make his final stand. Located 450 miles from Nadzab on Humbolt Bay and surrounded by 6,000-foot mountains and three airdromes, Hollandia contained most of what was left of Japan's air strength in New Guinea. To the south, Wewak was reportedly protected by 200,000 combat-hardened Japanese troops moved in from China. As it turned out, Hollandia was held by a huge force of mostly supply personnel.

Bypass and isolation became very effective fighting methods. At Wewak, two American infantry divisions assisting fine battle hardened Aussies bottled up the starving Japanese while air raids on Rabual by the Air Force and the Navy, along with constant attacks by torpedo boats, cut off the food and supply barges being brought to Wewak, immobilizing the Japanese and permitting our forces to hit bases farther north.

Aerial reconnaissance revealed that Hollandia's air strength consisted of 350 enemy planes on the three airstrips. In three days, that air force was destroyed by the 5th Air Force. Fighters knocked 50 of them out of the sky, and the rest were destroyed on the ground. Using these tactics isolated or eliminated 250,000 of enemy, preventing them from taking any further part in the war.

On these Hollandia raids, our planes came through with few losses but another enemy, that sweeping death-scythe called "tropical storm" cut down General Kenney's Air Force. The worst was "BLACK SUNDAY" 1944. Out of some 200 B-2, 4-, B-25, A-20 bombers and additional fighters that Kenney mustered that day, about 10% were lost.

Kenney's 5th Air Force lost 26. One report had it that 31 planes, returning from Hollandia short of fuel from the long flight, found the Markham River valley around Nadzab completely socked in by daytime-blackness. The planes couldn't be seen but we heard a few overhead and some in the distance, not realizing the awful fate to come to brave young men moments later. Some crews panicked. Some bailed out. Other planes flew around until they ran out of fuel, crashing where ever they were. Many crashed into the black shrouded mountains. General Kenney sadly related that it was the worst blow he took in the war.

Our jungle was home to pythons. Years before I had seen the "Bring 'Em Back Alive" movie made by Frank Buck. One scene featured a python that crawled into a pig's pen and swallowed a piglet whole. The bulge caused by the ingested pig kept the python a prisoner in the pen. I remembered that now, and I was determined from the first that Smoky should sleep tethered at the foot of my cot.

Scrub typhus, a disease caused by a tick that dogs could carry, presented a serious threat to us. It was said that this typhus killed nine out of ten who contracted it. Smoky was running free with me on walks in the jungle, and I encouraged her to chase small birds and butterflies (some bigger than she was) as a diversion from the intense training sessions.

This jungle exposure made the tick problem a more likely hazard. I decided she was to have a daily bath. Her tub was my helmet, which also served as my wash basin and a shaving sink. A natural part formed in Smoky's coat from the back of her neck to the tip of her tail when she shook off the water from her first bath. The almost dry hair fell straight down on both sides of her body. Brushing her hair back served no purpose because with another shake the strange part was back again. She was full of surprises.

I was working with a printing crew in the darkroom. Smoky came to the job with me. Outside, where the print washers and sorters were, she was a constant source of amusement, especially to Master Sergeant Irv Green, the lab chief. He came up with the idea of livening up the darkroom by placing the little dog in the tray used for passing wet photographs outside for washing in the daylight. Irv passed the tray through the light-trapped passage and listened as the usual banter picked up as Smoky was handed around by the printing crew. After a while, she was passed back again via the tray. Smoky spent most of the long days among her friends.

Playing "dead dog" became one of her favorite games. I would point my finger at her, shout, "BANG!" and she would fall down on her side. She was taught to lie very still, so I could poke her several times and she would remain still. Then, squatting down, I would pick her up by her hind legs, lift her and roll her over from hand to hand. As this was done, she would hang limp, dangling as though dead. Then I would place her back on the ground, poke her a few more times and through it all she remained "dead dog." I'd walk away and wait a bit. On command, "Okay," immediately brought her back to life. She would explode from her side onto her feet and charge to me. I don't know how she did this, but the little dog was praised loud and long for her good work.

About this time, "Yank Down Under" magazine (down under meant down under the equator) announced a contest to find the best mascots in the SWPA in two categories. The first was best mascot of a unit and the other was best mascot owned by an individual. Just about every outfit had some sort of pet, and many had more than one. Because we had been in the 26th for only a short time and another dog had come up from Australia with the squadron, it didn't seem right to nominate Smoky as a squadron mascot. However, the unit category would have fewer entrants, so it was the course I had to take.

To understand why "Yank" magazine would run such a contest, you have to realize how few hobbies and how little recreation were available to the soldiers in remote areas. Some constructed models of P-38s using copper sheets for wings and tails and empty 50-caliber machine gun cartridges for engines and tailbooms. Some collected the exotic butterflies native to New Guinea, where some of the world's most beautiful butterflies and some of the world's largest butterflies fly at low level (the Queen Alexandria has a 14-inch wing spread). Of course, we played baseball, basketball and volleyball. There were always card games: poker, gin rummy and pinochle, the most popular. We could visit native villages, write home or go to the movies every night and sit with the pouring rains running down our helmets and our ponchos. The mascot contest would be a pleasant diversion.

I wanted to come up with something different to attract the attention of the judges. A picture of Smoky in a GI helmet would emphasize her size, so I borrowed the lab's speed graphic 4-by-5 camera and shot it myself. My next wild idea was to have the dog make parachute jumps from a high tree at the ball field. I planned to have two people catch her in a GI blanket and to have someone else take pictures of her as she came down.

First, I needed to locate a pilot parachute, the small chute that opens first and pulls out the main chute when one bails out of an airplane. Parachute riggers Murphy and Piete provided one. Next, I made a harness out of money belts. Swinging her back and forth and up and down to get her accustomed to the new movement. As for the actual drop, a few new friends were enlisted to help. Don Esmond from Cleveland agreed to climb the tree and saw off enough branches on one side to give her a clear drop of about thirty feet. Howard Kalt, a staff sergeant would be the cameraman for the jumps. John Barnard and I would hold the blanket under the tree to catch our little chutist.

There was tension in the air as Esmond climbed the tree, dangling Smoky from the parachute. After we were in position for the photos and the catch and after the hot New Guinea wind had died down a bit, I yelled for the release. The dog, in her opened parachute, plummeted into the blanket, and we let out a cheer. Smoky wagged her tail gamely, so we sent her up again. Kalt snapped a picture of each jump.

We repeated the exercise until jump number six proved almost fatal. The wind caught the chute, collapsing it, and blew the dog out of the reach of our outstretched blanket. She arched her back, raising her behind higher than her front end and thrust out her front feet to break the fall.

She hit the foot-high grass, bounced two feet in the air and started yelping as she turned in circles with her head bent to the left. I raced to her, afraid of what I might have done to my innocent companion. Holding her down as she yelped and taking her head in one hand and her body in the other, I pulled on her gently until something that had seemed dislocated snapped back into place. She stopped spinning and whimpering as the guys gathered around her. She heaved up the canned wieners she had eaten earlier and remained uncharacteristically quiet. We wrapped her in the blanket. I was mad at myself for being foolish enough to risk her well-being with such a stunt. We all agreed that we were finished with that project.

When we got back to our tent, she was feeling much better. All night long I checked her for any change for the worse. I didn't know what I could do for her except search for a veterinarian at the Quartermaster Corps, where vets tested food for safety. But by daylight, Smoky was herself again.

Kalt wanted to take a picture of her on a 55-gallon gasoline drum. He pasted a cutout of that photo onto a picture of a cloud. With her ear-hair flying in the breeze, she looked like an aviator without a helmet. Her contest entry sheet stated that if the gang hadn't had a laugh all day, the sight of tiny Smoky chasing giant butterflies was enough to make anybody laugh.

CHAPTER 2

YANK'S CHAMP MASCOT

On rare occasions, Smoky broke free from her tether. I kept her tied to keep her from straying or from being stolen. Remembering the manner in which she was found, I feared she would get lost again. More than one GI said that if he saw that little mutt running around loose, he'd sure pick her up.

Once in a while, in spite of my precautions, I'd have to make a frantic search. Usually her excited yapping from the dense jungle behind our camp helped me to find her. She loved chasing wild hump-backed guinea hens. Little Smoky would battle her way through the tangled undergrowth with the hens running just in front of her. When I heard her yelping nearby, I'd call out, "Here they are! Here they are!" as I shook the tree limbs and made all kinds of ruckus. This usually brought her back to me out of curiosity. We'd play this way for a while and then she'd wag her tail as if to say, "Let's go! I know where lots of them are!"

One day after working late in the photo lab, I came back to the tent and Smoky was gone. I thought I heard her yapping in the distance and searched for half an hour to no avail. I was apprehensive and visions of stuffed pythons filled my head. Then I worried about the Papuans, who were no longer cannibals, but would be perfectly happy to eat a dog.

I spotted two natives walking along the jungle road and set out to enlist their help. In my best Pidgin English, I told them, "Me pella lose dog. You pella help find dog?"

Gesturing to describe her size and pointing to my hair to indicate the length of the dog's fur, I asked for help. They nodded that they understood and grinned widely, flashing their bright red betel-nut stained teeth. After they left, I heard them thrashing in the bush, and ten minutes later one of the Papuans burst through the snake-like vines carrying a squirming Smoky in his arms. I yelled a loud, "YAH!" Smiling, the black man nodded his head up and down. Before the native handed her back to me, he looked her over, rolling her around in his hand like a baseball. Then he passed her back to me, laughed, and said, "Smoky — Mary dog."

All women were called Mary. Baby girls were called Picka-ninny Mary. I had Smoky do a couple of tricks, and when they realized that the dog understood what I was saying, they seemed impressed.

17

Inter-squadron fast-pitch softball games were big events, attended by almost everyone, including the squadron mascots. During the warm-ups, as the players were tossing the ball around the bases and shagging flies, Smoky chased after every ball that came near her.

One evening we were playing a game against Wing Headquarters and Smoky was being held by someone along the third-base line. A quick grounder left the bat and Smoky shot like a rocket in pursuit of the ball. Just as the third baseman started to scoop up the ball, the dog caught up to it and was flipped into the air by the spinning grounder. She landed in the player's mitt, but the ball bounced between his wrists and legs. The puzzled fielder wasn't sure what had happened, but he managed to hold back from throwing the dog to second base.

We all had a good laugh as a shaken Smoky came back to the sidelines. "Wing Ding," the Wing's monthly bulletin, reported in its following issue, "O'Hara went to second on an error by Havel and Smoky, Lightning Dog Mascot."

Several days later, I developed a very high fever and the medics decided to hospitalize me. Leaving Smoky in the care of Frank Petrilak from Oliphant, Pennsylvania, I rode in the ambulance to the 3rd Field Hospital in Nadzab. This first-line hospital for combat troops consisted of tents held up by four tentpoles each—an arrangement similar to a circus setup.

My fever was raging at 105 degrees and they were loading me with sulfa. My malaria test came up negative, so it was decided that I must have Dengue Fever, which was also transmitted by mosquitoes.

We were all saturated with Atrabine, a drug designed to keep malaria from disabling military personnel and to keep them on their feet, fighting. On Atrabine, you might still have malaria but you wouldn't know it. Anyone who used it was left with a telltale yellow pallor. In Australia, those who had come from New Guinea loaded with this medicine were easily recognized.

My first full day in the hospital, I met a roomie who had arrived during the night. He was James Craig, a blond, curly-haired, smiling fellow with a thick New Jersey accent. His outfit was the 41st Division Combat Engineers. He had been hospitalized with pains in his chest, but a psychiatrist on Biak Island had diagnosed his real problem to be in his head. They had moved him over to Nadzab to check him out.

Along with the wounded, others were coming in suffering from combat fatigue. These soldiers dove out of bed and onto the floor every time they heard an explosion.

The taking of Biak Island became a necessary military goal. The three enemy airfields there must be ours if we were to move rapidly to the Philippines. The Hollandia airdromes lay on softer, rain-soaked ground, which had worked for the lighter enemy aircraft, but was unstable under the weight of our heavier bombers. MacArthur's aides realized they must take Biak, which was based on solid coral rock.

The Biak invasion was almost another disaster. About 11,000 Japanese troops were entrenched in the natural coral caves above the beach. These caves were an almost impenetrable natural defense for the Japanese. General Robert Eichelberger in his book, "The Jungle Road to Tokyo," describes the unique makeup of Biak Island:

> Caves intertwined so Japanese soldiers could disappear in the mouth of one cave and, passing through numerous underground caverns, reappear beyond ridges in another area. It was mind-boggling to the brass as well as the troops fighting to take positions. After taking them and moving forward, they would find the enemy rising up from caves behind them, causing our troops to fire on each other.

Eichelberger called off the battle to regroup and to set up a systematic way to eliminate this resistance. Both the number of troops and the nature of the fortifications had been underestimated by our forces.

Craig had been awarded the Legion of Merit for pulling some of his buddies away from exploding mortars in Hollandia.

When I had been in bed three days, Petrilak and Kalt brought Smoky to see me in the hospital tent. She greeted me excitedly. She had missed me as much as I had missed her. They also brought the mail, which included a large brown envelope from "Yank Magazine." It contained a copy of "Yank" and a letter:

"Dear PFC. Wynne:

I am enclosing herewith the first of your free copies of "Yank Down Under..."

"Wow!" I shouted. "We must have won!"

Before finishing the letter, I began paging through the magazine. There on Page 11, it read, "Smoky—FIRST PRIZE." At the top of the page, grinning at me from the helmet, was her impish majesty.

"First prize!" I yelled.

The friends looking over my shoulder were laughing as I continued reading the letter:

...which I trust you will enjoy reading. Each week for one year a copy of Yank Down Under will be mailed to you as a prize which your pet, Smoky, who won First Prize in our Mascot Contest, has been awarded. Thanking you for your interest in the Contest, I remain. Sincerely yours, Don E. Brewer, Sgt., Yank Down Under Contest Editor.

I was so thrilled that I didn't even feel sick any more.

Smoky became an instant heroine in the tent ward. The nurses asked if they could take her around to the other tent wards where a lot of wounded were still coming in from Biak and Wakde Islands. I was pleased that they asked. A major-doctor in charge of the 3rd Field Hospital stopped by and he decided Smoky could stay with me, on my bed. For the next five days, nurses took her around for visits with battle-weary GIs, presenting her as the "Champion Mascot of the SWPA."

When we returned from the hospital, we found our squadron making preparations to move to Hollandia. Our group was to be moved by air, except for trucks, cletracks for towing airplanes, and weapons carriers. Jeeps and all other equipment were to be flown by C-47 cargo planes, called Goonie Birds. The heavy equipment was to travel by boat from Lae, New Guinea with a small contingent of men. Before our departure, Ed Downey, whom I had not seen or heard from since we had both been transferred, came over to see Smoky. He was tickled to think that he had found her, and now she was getting famous. It was wonderful to see him again. Then, in July, I got another surprise. Kalt informed me that Colbert had just received a copy of "National Geographic" in the mail and that it proved that Smoky was a Yorkshire Terrier.

"A what?" I asked.

"A Yorkshire Terrier," he repeated. "The nickname is Yorkie. There is a picture of one in the magazine and it looks just like Smoky. Same color, short tail and long hair."

The "National Geographic," April, 1944, in an article entitled "Dogs in Toyland," carried a color photo of Suprema, a Yorkshire Terrier with a beautiful golden head, a gun-metal-blue body and glossy hair. The article said that the breed doesn't shed and if the hair, finer than human hair, is carefully wrapped in tissue, it can grow to a length of eighteen inches in five years. This, of course, was only for Yorkies entered in dog shows.

From the magazine's description, Smoky seemed to be a good standard of the breed, weighing just under four pounds. The article included a history of the Yorkies, recognized since 1886. They were bred for ratting in coal mines and were raised in the miners' kitchens. The natural part down her back was there on the dog in the picture, too. At one time, I thought perhaps she might be a Japanese breed and had taken her to an interpreter. She didn't respond to any of his words or commands, so the mystery had remained.

What kind of dog was she and how did she get to New Guinea? Now it was obvious this was a dog of people of means. I looked at her from my 6 feet to the distant bright eyes and blurry tail wagging. Smoky wasn't by any means a snooty dog at all. She had every right to be because she had CLASS. That was obvious from the Geographic article. But on the other hand nobody with real class is snooty. Her grace was like that charming human figure Audrey Hepburn arriving on the screen just shortly after. Extremely talented, captivating, everyone admitted she had an air of class. These were attributes these two shared. The graceful Smoky couldn't be denied despite the lack of a long flowing skirt or the trailing along of 8 inch sideburns and mustache of a seven inch Yorkie parading the show rings of the period. Or a crowning ribbon to hold her hair from her eyes. As a soldier Smoky's hair was bobbed. But what she had in common with most of all the show dogs from past to present was a splendid disposition.

One of my questions had now been answered. A YORKIE!

It was time to move from Nadzab leaving behind some losses to the squadron. Captain Sheldon P. Hallett, our former operations officer, was listed as missing in action when his plane was downed off the coast of New Guinea. First Lieutenant Donald W. Christians was killed making a forced landing at Saidor, New Guinea. Lieutenant William McDaniels and our sergeant major, T/Sgt. Harry R. Rogers crashed and died in Madang Harbor in a P-38 piggy back, a modified single-place plane that allowed a passenger to crouch behind the pilot. They were on an administrative mission.

Our advance echelon, consisting of two officers and five enlisted men, were the first Air Corps personnel to land in the Admiralties.

At this point, we also had men and planes stationed on Manus and Wakde Islands.

Not wanting to take my dog to Hollandia by ship, I asked Lieutenant William Bishop, one of our most popular pilots, to fly Smoky to Hollandia and give her to my friend, John Barnard, who would keep her until I arrived. Lieutenant Bishop agreed.

Before we could get the ship loaded at Lae, we were caught in a deluge that had us scrambling for higher ground as the rain-swollen Markham River flooded to our cot tops.

The squadron camped temporarily between the mountains and the airfield near Lake Sentani. Our next move would be to Biak, where more than 5000 enemy soldiers were still holding out around what was to be our squadron area. Because we were planning to move so quickly, no shower was set up. We bathed in the fast mountain stream that ran through the area. Barnard reported to me that Smoky had found a boy friend while she was running around loose on the island. I didn't believe him.

Dr. Beryl D. Rosenburg, the squadron doctor, returned from furlough and offered me a recuperative leave to Brisbane, Australia. I took my orders for 15 days leave, packed Smoky in my musette bag and hitchhiked a ride on a C-47 to Port Moresby. Instead of taking the regular route back to Nadzab and then through the pass to Port Moresby, this pilot took off in the rain and, because of the poor visibility, barely cleared the forests and headed out over the jungle.

We were overloaded with two radial engines in crates and ten infantrymen in full gear. (Goonies were redlined at 5,000 pounds cargo weight.) The crew chief came back as we lifted off and asked me to come up front to the pilots cabin because the plane was tail heavy. Several others had to move forward to the wing area. We made it safely to Port Moresby, but not without some apprehension.

On our next flight, to Townsville, Australia, Smoky and I traveled with six sailors on leave from their PT boat. As we deplaned I felt freezing cold, although the temperature was about 80 degrees. This was quite a change from the equatorial heat. The first thing we all asked for was fresh milk. Only those deprived of that basic drink for eight months can really appreciate it. Fresh meat was another luxury we were looking forward to.

Even covered by the six woolen blankets we had been issued. Smoky and I shivered all night. The next morning, during a visit to a hobby shop, I found a green wool felt card table cover with beading stitched around the outside. At the Red Cross, we located volunteers working on sewing machines for the service men (usually sewing stripes and insignia on new uniforms issued for the men's leaves).

They made a blanket for Smoky by fitting her and cutting the material to go across her back from neck to tail. A band to close the front was stitched on and the beading from the table cloth was sewed around the whole edge of the blanket. Two cloth ties were added underneath. A 5th Air Force patch was sewn on along with corporal's stripes, in honor of our new rank. A US insignia and a small brass propeller button (used on enlisted men's blouses), a triangular photo patch, two six-months-overseas bars, an Asiatic Pacific Ribbon and a Good Conduct Ribbon completed the decorations.

Because of bad weather conditions, we were grounded the next day, so we went to town with several others scheduled for rest leave in Brisbane. We were surprised by the lack of automobiles and by the little horse-drawn wagons moving about in the streets. The most memorable part of the visit was the "Stike and Eyeggs" we had for breakfast. Eager to get out of our GI boots, we headed for a shoe store. The clerk was so amused by Smoky's antics that she let us purchase shoes without ration stamps, something unheard of in those times.

We had an indication of how popular the Yorkie was going to be when we approached a "casket" line. People betting on that day's horse races waited in this line outside a tavern that sold betting tickets.

"Look at the Yank with the silkie!" someone shouted, and the laughing crowd formed a semi-circle around us. To protect her, I gathered Smoky into my arms.

"Give the silkie to me," a woman pleaded. "I'll take good care of it."

I smiled. "Couldn't part with her ma'am," I replied leaving in a hurry.

Later, In Brisbane, we arrived at the American Red Cross Riverside, housed in a large building with free sleeping quarters and excellent food.

After we had been in Brisbane a few days, some people came to ask me if I would mind taking Smoky to the 109th Fleet Naval Hospital to visit sailors and Marines. Wounds do not heal well in the tropics. If, in this semi-tropical part of Australia, the healing process was still too slow, the injured were sent back to the States. Meanwhile, a little entertainment was a real morale booster.

That hospital was the first place we put on our show. We did eight wards that day and the patients loved it. Smoky performed her obedience trials, played dead (which had them rolling in the aisles—figuratively) and, of course, she sang. She had learned a new trick, the grapevine, where she passed through and around my legs as we walked along quickly. This one was always the show-stopper.

Barbara Wood Smith, the Red Cross lady who invited us to the hospital, asked if I would let the newspaper do a story about Smoky. Knowing that Australia had strict quarantine laws and knowing that I had pretty much smuggled her in, I chose not to okay any publicity. We continued to entertain all sorts of people there at the Red Cross facilities. One of the volunteers decided that Smoky was a Red Cross worker and should have an ARC pin. She removed one from her collar and pinned it on the dog's blanket. Two days later, a WAC, noting the ARC pin, said, "If Smoky is a female in the Army, she must be a WAC," and she fastened her lapel button to the blanket.

Next, Barbara asked if I would bring Smoky to the U.S. 42nd General Army Hospital in Brisbane. There we performed and talked with the GIs in twelve wards. In each ward, I told them how I got Smoky and about her winning the "Yank" contest as best mascot in the SWPA. These guys were starved for entertainment and we got a big hand wherever we went. The joy and speed with which the little dog worked enchanted them, as it did the millions who saw her during her lifetime. That day, GIs in wheelchairs followed us from ward to ward, some asking to hold her, some asking what I fed her.

My answer was always the same, "Regular mess hall chow, Spam, bully beef, Australian canned mutton and, occasionally, vitamin pills."

Barbara wrote a thank you letter addressed to Smoky, calling her "a lady artiste without temperament."

While in Brisbane, I stopped in at "Yank Magazine" and saw the editor. When he heard that we had never received the silver loving cup that he had sent through the mail two months before, he telephoned Hardy Brothers, Goldsmiths to the King, and ordered another cup. The engraving read:

SMOKY
First Prize Yank Mascot
Australia 1944

CHAPTER 3

SMOKY'S SURPRISE

It was a real sweat returning north to the squadron, now on Biak Island. This coral rock battleground was 25 miles long and only four degrees south of the equator. We heard the rumors of typhus-carrying ticks on the island and I wondered if dogs were allowed. My driver told me on the phone that another dog and her pup were already there. Actually, there was no scrub typhus on Biak, but several islands across the bay had reported some cases.

The photo lab was going 24 hours a day when I arrived. Our 12-hour shifts were once again interrupted by air raid alarms, which sent us scurrying into the caves abandoned by the Japanese. Day and night we headed for these caves. Sometimes we heard bombs whooping in the distance. Some 5,000 Japanese troops remained scattered on the island, mostly inland.

My tent was on a line dividing the 25th and 26th Photo Squadrons, and Frank Petrilak was my tent mate. Our 8x10 shelter was about 50 feet from the photo lab, and we listened to printing crews talking all through the night shifts. We didn't always have 24-hour shifts, but we did for spells when there were big military pushes.

Many days it was impossible to fly because of the weather and sometimes planes were grounded for several weeks. Actually, what we had was some free time to swim in the ocean. The tides rolling in and out filled a large bomb crater (24 feet in diameter) with water about four feet deep. Whenever Smoky got loose she headed, running and barking, for the beach to chase small birds. She never got close, but the birds learned to lead her to the bomb crater for a daily dunking. She always paddled her way across the water to resume the chase. Invariably, her playful feathered prey took her back around for another swim. As bright as she was, she never figured out their little game.

Because the salt water was hard on her hair, she needed a freshwater bath after these dunkings. We used half a helmetful for the bath, another half for the rinse. Her spirit was never damped by the horrid living conditions. One could remember living in a nice if old house where temperatures were lower, with carpets for a dog to lie on. This Yorkie had a hot air-cooled tent home. The ocean 75 yards away offered the cooling 95 degree breezes. One hundred and 130 degrees in the tents were common. Her carpet generally was hard coral white rock formed by centuries of washing sea waves bringing the gathered minute sea animals growing first into reefs and then islands. Vegetation was scarce. Luckily a little grass was in the tent. But stunted shrub trees and tall coconut palms prevailed. Our palms had their heads blown off by naval guns. Under my cot was an added protected roof for Smoky.

Overall this little dog took the rough conditions better than her human companions. She was never sick with dysentery, malaria, dengue fever, yellow jaundice or any dog diseases either. Because of her good health we could at any time play by going to the beach to chase birds.

One of Smoky's more roughneck playmates was Colonel Turbo, the rhesus monkey mascot of the 25th Photo Recon Squadron. When the two animals met for the first time, a pal bragged that Turbo would mangle our little dog. "He can handle anything," he said. Turbo had been the runner-up in the" Yank Down Under" contest.

This monkey was a legend in the South Pacific. He had been purchased from a zoo in Raton, New Mexico, where the squadron had been on maneuvers prior to their overseas assignment. The pilot who had bought him was killed in a plane crash, and the squadron's sentiments were that Turbo should be kept on. Sgt. Bice adopted him and the unit stuck by their mascot in spite of his nasty ways. (Turbo's service record included his time inducted into the squadron, shot records and the battle stars and other citations his unit received.) He was a biter who either liked you or not, and you knew which it was immediately because you had the tooth marks to verify it.

Apparently his grouchiness was the result of bad handling. When the 25th was ready to be shipped overseas, they gave Turbo sleeping pills for two days. He staggered around groggily until time to board ship and then he was stuffed in a barracks bag and smuggled aboard. During inspection, he was hung out the porthole on a leash where he clung to a three-inch ledge, three decks above the sea. After inspection, he was hauled back in.

Their first stop was in New Zealand. Turbo was taken ashore by his buddies, but the Kiwi customs officials sent them right back to the ship. Their liberty was cancelled because they had violated the quarantine laws. That was Turbo's first payback.

He was a real devil when he worked himself loose. He went from tent to tent, ripping open cigarette cartons, shredding cigarettes, opening packages from home, eating the goodies and rummaging through everyone's bags. A tornado never left a worse trail of debris. He was generally hated, but kept for sentimental reasons and his sometimes-entertaining ways and because no one had the heart to shoot him! Once when he was biting on a high-tension wire, several fellows egged him on, hoping he would bite through the coating. Occasionally his companions tried to lose him in the jungle by freeing him and then jumping onto their fleeing truck. He always found his way back to his squadron, bouncing into camp with his side-waddle three-legged hop.

Turbo was very crafty with dogs. His favorite trick was to put his head on the ground and raise his hips in the air, tucking his hands back between his legs. When the dog came sniffing, he grabbed the dog's front legs and wrestled him to the ground. He could then best any dog by biting him and pulling his ears until he yelped in pain. Smoky was very touchy, but took on animals much larger than herself. I was wary of letting her tangle with Turbo, but I was sure that Turbo never really hurt his victims—just roughed them up a bit.

On the day of their confrontation, I set Smoky on the ground near Turbo's tiedown post. She walked over to check him out. He grabbed her by the nose! She backed off and yelped in surprise, then lunged forward to grab the husky monkey. Turbo tried to catch her, but she was too fast for him. She charged at him, snapping, and skinned his nose. He jumped into his tree and rubbed the spot she had nicked, checking his hand for bleeding.

By this time a crowd had gathered. Smoky turned her back to the monkey, so he sneaked down from his protective perch to grab her tail. Whirling around, she flew at him again, squealing as if he were pulling her hair out! The high-pitched squeal and her quick assault had Turbo desperate to find his tree again.

Flinching at each snap and literally at the end of his rope, Turbo could do nothing but jump into the air attempting to stay out of her reach. Each time he hit the ground, he couldn't get back into the air fast enough or high enough. Finally, he made it to his tree and safety. It was the first time the great dog-mauler had ever been on the run himself. The gang was roaring with laughter. When someone tried yanking on the leash to get Turbo back into the match, he bared his teeth and threatened this tormenter.

From then on, when Smoky tired of chasing little birds, she sought out her other playmate, Turbo, whose home tent was just a few yards away from hers. Theirs was a cautious friendship, and the monkey was never able to bully her as he did the other dogs.

The new NCO club occasionally had supplies brought up from Australia in a B-25 Mitchell bomber. Pilots were using this plane to log instrument-flying time, and it was not unusual for this blind flying to take them to the mainland. The plane, stripped of armor plate and guns, afforded space for carrying fresh meat, more than 20 cases of liquor and several barrels of coke syrup. Often this cargo was too voluminous to load in the bomb bay and still get the doors closed. So, the doors were left open with the barrels hanging out less than a foot above the runway on take-offs and landings. These planes, which did so much to elevate our lifestyle, were appropriately called Fat Cats.

Shortly after the 26th Photo arrived on Biak, an infantry patrol came by looking for volunteers to assist in a mopping-up exercise. First Sgt. J.B. Howell volunteered. His plan was to test out this clean-up of enemy forces before allowing others to volunteer. Three days later, he returned with six notches in his Ml Garand and harrowing tales of combat. He told of being pinned down behind a fallen tree for two hours, waiting for the patrol to get back to rescue him. His narrative prompted our executive officer, Capt. McCullough, to call for a squadron formation.

Getting right to the heart of things, as always, Capt. Mac drawled in his thick Louisiana accent

"Men, theah will be no moah 26th men pahmitted to go on infantry pahtrol. If we lost anaone, it'd be damned difficult ta explain ta Headquahters how a Ayah Corps man was lost moppin' up. Besides ah'm not shoah the rest of ya all is as tough as Howell is. Squadron dismissed!"

At this point, the photo lab was again being pressed into round-the-clock, seven-day-a-week service, knocking out thousands of negatives and tens of thousands of prints. Later, the 26th Photo received its first Presidential Unit Citation for outstanding coverage of the Philippine Islands, September 18-20, 1944.

To escape the war routines and relieve my boredom, I continued to pursue my dog-training hobby. One of my most ambitious projects was to teach my little pal to walk a tight-rope, blindfolded. Sgt. Gil Frankhuizen, a sheet-metal expert, made a couple of pipe T's, four feet in length and a six inch piece tacked on top. Then he welded two 4x6 inch plates on each T. The plates served as platforms and were torch-cut from steel oil drums. These uprights were set as stanchions in the coral rock. Two aircraft control cables were stretched between them and fastened at angles to the ground. We installed the cables 2 1/2 inches apart, then drew them tightly between the platforms and down to spikes driven into the coral. They were tightened by aircraft turnbuckles.

I began Smoky's training by setting her on the wires to teach her to keep her balance. Then I slowly urged her to walk across, holding her firmly with the leash and steadying her with my hand on her back. Sgt. Green watched with some amusement from the door of the photo lab as she slowly gained her confidence. The next day we repeated this routine, first on the leash, then off, and after some time, the little dog moved with assurance.

It was time to try the blindfold. She put her nose deep between the wires and I held her tight on the leash. With my encouragement, she soon mastered the feat. Smoky was a blindfolded wire-walker! We needed a ladder, so Frankhuizen made a short one with inch-wide steps set four inches apart. We attached it to the platform and she learned to climb up and down the ladder. Because this was a lot of work for her, we practiced mostly on cooler evenings.

Next, I taught her to walk on a barrel. We practiced with a 55-gallon metal oil drum. After placing her on the drum, once again using the leash for guidance, I slowly rolled the drum with my foot, letting her propel her feet on top. Before long, she could, on command, jump on and off the drum, without the leash.

As complex as all this training sounds, working with such an intelligent dog made it a pleasure. For me, the only drawback was the heat on Biak. Temperatures during the day were usually over 100 degrees. It was so hot that even a slow walk could produce heavy perspiration. We took many siestas, trying to rest as much as possible between noon and 2 p.m.

One day Smoky behaved strangely during her barrel walk. She refused to continue the routine, rolling over on her back instead. I put the leash back on and scolded her severely for her disobedience. It did no good. I took her back to our tent and plunked her down on the cot. As I tried to figure out what had gone wrong, there before my astonished eyes, she presented me with a small black object.

"HOLY CATS! IT'S A PUPPY!" I yelled.

You could have knocked me over with a feather! A couple of the guys ran over to see what all the excitement was about. There it was, a little damp black ball and, like any good mother. Smoky was cleaning him up for his debut. I ran outside, wondering if she might have dropped another while I was forcing her to walk the barrel. There were no others.

Unfortunately, the arrival of the puppy cost Smoky her good conduct medal and a year of good behavior would pass before she had earned it back. We decided that Duke, John Hembury's small mixed-breed terrier, had been her paramour. Duke was a native of Nadzab; his mother, an Australian.

For days after the big event, GIs came from all around the area to see a puppy born of a dog that weighed less than four pounds herself. Among her callers was Jim Craig, my old pal from the Nadzab field hospital. He had heard about Smoky's pup and wanted to see it.

After discovering that we had Coca Cola at the enlisted men's club, he visited even more frequently. Coke syrup, water and compressed air from an aircraft oxygen tank produced our coveted beverage. The mixture generated a fizz that didn't do well in aluminum canteens, but I had one of the few canteens and cups coated with black enamel. Jim and I raised many a toast to Smoky and her little surprise. The first time the mention of her name caused her to perk up, and she joined in the toast with a sharp bark.

CHAPTER 4

ADVENTURES OF WAR

In late August, I was offered the opportunity to get the required 300 combat hours that would allow me to return to the States sooner. I was eligible for combat flying because I had attended aerial photo school. T/Sgt. Les Switzer was the official aerial photographer of the squadron, but two photographers were needed for missions. I agreed to go, hoping that I could get home earlier and that my rating would be raised from corporal to staff sergeant. Orders putting the two of us on flying status came through on September 16, 1944.

A young lieutenant from the 3rd Emergency Rescue Squadron needed a photographer to fly with him to check on the status of a pilot who had crashed over enemy lines. If he had survived and if we could locate him, an infantry patrol might be able to rescue him. About 5,000 of the enemy remained scattered throughout Biak. Although somewhat disorganized, they still presented a clear challenge to would-be rescuers.

I climbed into my summer flying coveralls, put on the shoulder holster carrying my .45-caliber automatic, took an extra clip of bullets and some birdshot, and packed my Bowie knife. We took off for the Sorido airstrip. Our Stinson L-5, slightly larger than a Piper Cub, seemed ridiculously small.

Buzzing off, we cleared the ridge in front of us, banked around and immediately flew over no-man's land. Staying at 800 feet, we flew over ridges and valleys of white coral and scrub tree growth until we reached a flatter area, where the pilot took us down to 50 feet. Scanning the ground below, I saw a number of holes, about four feet in diameter. Their thatched palm roofs, mounted on poles, were somewhat askew. With his engine barely idling, the pilot yelled back to me, "See those damned things down there?"

"Ya," I shouted back.

"Those are Jap foxholes," he shouted.

Imagining small arms fire hitting me in the seat of my pants, I pleaded, "Let's get out of here."

"You don't have to worry," he continued, "we bombed those out yesterday."

"Bombed them?" I asked.

"We dropped hand grenades on them," he said, smiling.

We continued the slow flight until we came to a mound with a large crater. At its base an Allison engine sitting. Pieces of aluminum were scattered about and we saw a skid line too short to indicate a safe landing. We circled three times while I took pictures with the K24 aerial camera. The lieutenant turned to tell me there was another P-38 nearby. The plane was intact but the cockpit section of the fuselage had been ripped off by a tree. The poor guy hadn't had a chance.

I photographed the crash site and we headed for the ocean. There, submerged in shallow waters, was a Zero in perfect condition. That pilot had probably survived. We returned to the base with 35 minutes of combat time logged. Combat time is defined as time spent "where enemy fire is probable and expected."

Back at the 26th, several guys gathered around to hear about the mission. Jack Crays, from a neighboring tent, asked, "Hey, Wynne, if you get knocked off, I can have Smoky, can't I?" Petrilak piped up, "No, I get her!" Others laid claim to her, too.

I replied, disgustedly, "From now on, she goes with me. If it happens, we go down together!"

Several days later, 1st Lieutenant Clair J. Bardsley failed to return from a flight to Ambon. In Nadzab, Bardsley and I had played in a basketball contest. After eliminating 13 others, only he and I remained. It was well after dark when he missed a shot and I was declared the winner.

My next missions were flown in Catalina PBY-5As, nicknamed Cats, Army designation OA-10. One morning at 2:00 a.m., I was driving over to the 3rd ERS without headlights. The road in front of me seemed to be in constant movement, making me almost seasick. Thousands of hermit crabs were migrating, crossing the road in undulating masses.

When we reached the ERS, I breakfasted on fried eggs and salty bacon. Smoky had to settle for eggs. The bacon would have made her too thirsty during the upcoming flight. (Fresh eggs were always broken at arms' length just in case their freshness had been overrated.)

The heavy canvas musette bag I used as Smoky's hiding place, had two tie-down straps with buckles to close it tightly. In a bailout, I planned to fasten the bag's strap around my waist and then deploy the parachute.

During the pre-flight briefing, we were reminded to try to land our planes near the coastline if we were hit. We were also told to be cautious about jungle villagers. Some were unfriendly and some cannibalistic. Villages were run by "number one boys," those who were physically strongest. They kept their position by beating up challengers. The natives generally supported our cause, but there were some who were friendly to the Japanese. Three surviving crewmen of a 90th Bomb Group squadron were known to have been eaten by a tribe in Dutch New Guinea.

Our assignment was to search for Clair Bardsley. One of our squadron's pilots had seen him over the target at Ambon. We didn't know if he had been shot down or had suffered an accident. Our crew consisted of a pilot, co-pilot, navigator, engineer-mechanic, radio operator and two medic waist-gunners. I was to ride in the waist at the big window blisters with a .50 caliber machine gun on it's post turned to the side. All nine of us plus a hidden dog loaded into a jeep with equipment, lunches, parachutes, aerial camera and driver. We were so crowded that the chauffeur couldn't see to drive, so someone up front verbally guided him along the road.

We arrived at the plane at 3:00 a.m. With ourselves and our equipment safely aboard, we rolled down the coral-white runway and soared off into the dark. The medics were amused when they discovered our canine stowaway and heard my reason for bringing her along. They hung her bag out of the way, over a nearby stretcher.

Although our missions were primarily rescue, the 3rd ERS planes had no red cross markings, only the standard markings of an American battle plane. The medics doubled as gunners, manning the .50-caliber machine guns located in the waist blisters.

We headed for Ceram, west of the New Guinea coast. At daylight, we settled at low altitude, cruising at 90 mph. Because we were friends, Bardsley's fate was important to me, so I scanned the surface with intensity. The sweeps produced no results. We saw no evidence of life on the sea.

Suddenly, dark clouds formed and we were in the midst of a fierce squall, being buffeted, pitched and dropped. We climbed to 12,000 feet, but were unable to rise above the storm. Down at 100 feet was no better, and for four hours, we were unable to see the wing tips, but our magnificent navigator kept us on a steady course and, somehow, got us home. Over Biak Island, the weather was clear.

Smoky and I continued flying with a variety of crews. One mission covering a strike to Borneo was particularly risky. We took off in the PBY at 3:00 a.m. The bombers were scheduled to leave at 5:00 a.m. and the fighters at 7:00. The sequence was ordered according the speed of the planes, the slowest leading off. After we took off, bad weather closed in and the other flights never got into the air. Hours later we were over the target, the Balikpapan oil fields, all alone. We got out of there just as fast as we could.

When flying in groups, Australians, Americans and other allies with fewer planes used the Cats (sometimes called Black Cats) very effectively. Japanese war historians claim the PBYs sank 700,000 tons of shipping, 10 percent of their total naval losses. Some Cats alternated between bombing missions and rescue patrols. More than 1,600 fliers from the Fifth Air Force were saved by cats.

Single planes were to stay out to sea on standby, ready to fly in if Dumbo (code for PBYs) got a rescue call. A SNAFU call meant there was a downed plane with possible survivors. MAYDAY was the call from a plane going down. If fighter cover was available, they came in. If not, the Cat crew took its chances, dropping life rafts and heading down for a water landing. The medics, using a rubber raft, sometimes rowed to the survivors, pulling them back to the plane and in through the blisters. If a downed man had a raft, he rowed over to the plane.

Back on base, Smoky's pup was growing and in good health. Frank Petrilak adopted him and named him Topper. I was back to just one dependent.

I thought maybe I could teach Smoky to ride a scooter, so I constructed one. Using my jungle knife, I carved a half-inch-thick orange crate end into a 12-inch-long scooter. Small hard-fiber pulleys with good roller bearings served nicely as the wheels. These had been used previously for moving airplane control cables.

Necessity is said to be the mother of invention. My constant needs in training Smoky led to the birth of a number of inventions. The only one of Smoky's tricks that I had seen performed before was the wire-walking. As an 11-year-old, I had been amazed by it at a department store Christmas show. I had tried to teach some of the tricks to another dog, with little success. Now here I was, inventing as I went along, teaching my little friend strictly by trial and error. Here was this unbelievable dog, her head of bright shining gold with matching gold legs, the silver-blue body and stubby tail which, when she pranced stood almost, but not quite upright. And underneath all that golden hair on her head was a massive thinking mind. A room sized computer was crammed into that ridiculous baseball sized head. How could it think so fast? But the real mystery was, how could it hold so much?

When my dog, Pal, had disappeared back in Cleveland, I was so heartsick that I vowed never again to be that close to anyone—animal or human. But Smoky, the little tyke who shared so much with me, who, unquestioning and courageously, responded to my every command, had become my truest friend. She was a diversion from the demoralizing reality of war. She made us laugh and forget. The thought that it could all end suddenly was sobering, so, as we flew together on combat missions, I was ready for the worst but remained determined within all my power to keep her safe. We were a team.

Smoky continued to bounce along with us, her bag hung over the bunks in the PBYs. On mission days, she ate only one meal. I felt her back, stomach and ribs daily to determine the amount of her food and adjusted it regularly to her waist size. Smoky had a ravenous appetite and would have eaten everything in sight all the time if I had not watched her. I kept her a bit on the hungry side, and that turned out to be the best regimen for her. She was a healthy, active little dog.

During long flights, I let her run around for a while on the upper bunk, but not long enough for her to relieve herself. Several of these missions lasted seemingly endless hours, and she was not always comfortable on these flights. Victor Kregel, a pilot now living in Colorado Springs, Colorado, remembers Smoky shivering on several fights. The endless drone of the engines, along with their continuous vibration, put her into a nervous state at times. Her panting tongue sometimes turned a deep red color.

This was not unlike pets today riding in baggage compartments of commercial airlines which may be similarly uninsulated against cold and noise causing the animals similar stress. She was also very sensitive to the crew's anxieties. Most of the time, though, she was finally able to relax and sleep soundly, wrapped in her wool blanket at higher altitudes. On the ground, she reacted tensely to the air alerts and barked loudly as we scrambled for our foxhole.

To some, it may seem that I was cruel to her, taking her on combat flights. But, historically, dogs have been at man's side in warfare. Dogs were serving side by side with GIs all over the world, as sentries, cable layers and guard dogs. More than 500,000 dogs were used in World War II.

35

The dogs had nothing to say about their participation, but they remained as companions to the men they served, often dying at their masters' sides. I, too, asked my companion to serve with me.

It was really cruel of me to ask my little friend to hang in a musette bag for hours on end several times as long as 20 hours with no chance to relieve herself. Smoky would look out through the bag flap and lick my hand when I petted her. But together we must survive or die. A man's decision a poor one perhaps, but then again the hazards of war were all about us in the air or on the ground, many were killed or injured merely riding in ground vehicles. It was never as safe as riding under the worse conditions on streets or roads back in the states. My resolve was to protect her the best I could and get her home with me after this was over.

Flying with us as cover on several of our missions were two top P-38 pilots, Major Richard I. Bong, with 40 enemy planes shot down, and Major Thomas McGuire, with 38 to his credit before he died.

During some down time, a couple of enlisted men built a bellytank boat. Two obsolete drop tanks, three feet apart were lashed to poles and topped with a wooden platform. The ten foot mast boasted a discarded parachute which served as a sail. A large hole cut in the top of each tank formed a cockpit. One fine day, Frank Petrilak and Jack Tankersly invited me for a sail. Tankersly had the experience. Frank and I were landlubbers. The idea was to sail a bit on the bay and then visit a native village. I put Smoky in one of the cockpits and we pushed out to sea. There was little breeze, so we paddled a bit from the cockpits as the man up on the deck controlled the rudder. The water was smooth as glass as we moved away from the shore. Our craft was amateurish, built with crude materials and no quality control, and, thus, with no guarantees.

The wind picked up and we moved more briskly under sail. Suddenly, Smoky jumped out of the boat, into the water, and began swimming for shore. We were a half mile out and my first thought was that the dog would become shark bait! I dived in after her and caught her about 25 feet away and, holding her out of the water, sidepaddled back to the boat. We had not seen any sharks, but we knew they were in the bay.

With Smoky safely on board, we continued our voyage. We landed at the tip of the bay where the land jutted out farthest. We were invited to enter a native house, a little hut mounted on stilts over the water. The inside was furnished with uncovered bamboo beds and little else. Both sexes here wore sarongs, but one woman was wearing a University of Wisconsin T-shirt. Smoky was entertaining the native boys with her

36

crab-chasing antics. As a crab crawled along, Smoky pounced on it, then growled and spun around a couple of times. The crab ducked, then crawled away a bit before Smoky pounced on it again and then repeated her strange crustacean dance.

We noticed the sky darkening and heavy clouds hanging over-head, so we decided to hurry home. We pushed our boat out over the coral reef into deeper water. A strong wind caught our sail and dunked the nose of our bellytanks under water. Petrilak started bailing. I jumped to the back of the tanks, hoping my weight would keep the bows high. The wind grew even stronger, the waves swelled higher and Tankersly tried to tack us toward shore. He admitted he had never tried anything like this back home. We struck the reef, banging dents in our tanks, and began to take on more water. The boat was coming apart. I tried jumping into the water to push the boat off the reef and into the sea. We were not in any real danger, but we hoped to get the boat back in one piece.

Once we were free of the reef, the wind drove us at a fast clip. In a conventional ship, the sailors could drop the sail and sea anchor and ride out the storm. But our cockpits were open to the sea and we had no air tanks to keep us afloat if we were swamped, so we had no choice but to keep bailing and sailing. Our wrestling match with the sea lasted two hours, but we finally made it back to the squadron area. We found eight guys who had been watching our battle through field glasses.

Smoky had swallowed some sea water. After wiping her down, I covered her with a heavy towel. Our usual nighttime temperature was around 90 degrees, but this night it was only 75 degrees and we were cold. Some of the larger tents had been blown down in the wind, but ours was still standing. Looking back, I sometimes wonder if Smoky sensed the oncoming storm and tried to swim back home before it struck.

One morning at 3:00, we were about to board the plane for another 13-hour flight, when Smoky, off the leash to relieve herself, dashed full speed across the runway and into the dark. I took off after her and caught her about 500 feet away. I scolded her and we climbed the ladder into the blister. The crew was silent and somewhat apprehensive. Was it a bad omen to have the little dog run away from the Cat? We usually thought of her as a good luck charm. Who knows. Maybe she delayed us long enough for us to avoid some danger. Our flight passed without incident— not even a weather problem. Combat crews sometimes become a bit superstitious.

On an afternoon in mid-October, we were returning from the Philippines when, looking down through patchy clouds, we caught sight of a huge convoy, a veritable armada heading in the opposite direction. The parade of ships seemed endless. They had to be ours or we would have been knocked out of the sky. We were soon challenged by a pair of Navy Corsairs. The Cat acknowledged the challenge with quick dips of our right wing. Although we were marked American, there was always the possibility that we were a captured plane being flown by the enemy the wing dips were our code of "friendly." I don't remember the number of columns I saw, but there were battleships, carriers, cruisers, destroyers and an endless array of troop carriers and other smaller ships. It took more than half an hour for us to pass this convoy headed for Leyte Gulf. (Leyte was where MacArthur first returned to the Philippines.) Those Corsairs were the only planes I had ever seen on any of our lonely flights.

Back at the base, I inquired about the possibility of a promotion. No chance, I was told. They did offer me combat leave if I wanted it. I had flown 73 hours on 13 missions in 10 weeks, and I was ready for some R and R. Smoky was ready, too, so I packed our bags for a 10-day leave and we were off to Sydney in a Transport Command C-47.

I was swapping war stories with some of the Jolly Roger 90th Bomber Group, also on leave. They were recounting the close calls they had. The closest call I ever had came on the second day I was overseas. In Brisbane, five of us were huddled in a shower shelter, hoping to escape the wind and rain of a storm, when a great tree came down on top of us. We were all thrown to the ground and I landed on my haunches, hands between my legs. I bounced up, miraculously unhurt. The others were seriously injured.

A short tail-gunner from the 90th looked me right in the eye and, pointing his finger at me, shouted, "You are being saved for a bullet!"

Once in Sydney, Smoky and I shared a room with another gunner. Our elderly landlady wanted to let us use the room rent free, but we gave her two pounds each. Normally, dogs were not allowed in the building; however. Smoky was tiny and the landlady liked her, so we were permitted to stay. I smuggled Smoky out in the musette bag for her daily exercise in a nearby park. She never made a sound anywhere we stayed as long as she had a shirt or cap of mine to lie next to. She knew I would always return.

Walking down a main street in Sydney one morning almost cost me my dog. We were practicing heeling off the leash. When I looked down to see how she was doing. Smoky was gone! Turning around, I spotted a woman hurrying in the other direction with Smoky's tail and hind legs sticking out beneath her elbow. I dashed up to her, grasped her arm and said, "Pardon me ma'am, but you've got my dog."

"No 'e isn't, Yonk. 'E's m' silkie, 'e is! 'E was walkin' by and ah picked 'im up, ah did," she stated boldly.

"She's been mine for a long time in New Guinea, ma'am. You'd better give her back to me—right now!" I shouted, drawing the attention of passersby. She handed Smoky back to me. We turned away and continued our walk, but that incident ended my practice of heeling her off the leash in Australia.

CHAPTER 5

LUZON INVASION

There was an air of nervous anticipation in the squadron when we returned from Australia. But, we still had some time to let down. We had fresh turkey, cranberries and pumpkin pies for Christmas. At our New Year's Eve party, a liberal supply of the best available alcoholic beverages was brought to us in the B-25 by an enthusiastic Captain John Brown. The party was well attended and most of our carbines were fired at midnight.

Brown later recounted, "The greatest flight I was ever on was when Buck Buchanan and I took the B-25 (fat cat) down to the Navy base in Manus Island with all the money we had. We bought 505 cases of beer, made in Minneapolis, Minnesota."

In the middle of all this activity, we were loading the LST 927 for the invasion of Luzon. The squadron members detached to other bases had returned. We were informed of orders grounding all flying personnel except for those needed to fly our F-5s up to the next station.

The 26th was the only photo recon squadron going to Luzon. We were placed under the command of General Krueger and the 6th Army. No letters home were permitted. All the supplies and equipment had to be backed up the ramp and through the open doors of the LST. Then they had to be stacked deep in the tank deck. It was back-breaking, as usual.

The excitement of the move was somewhat tempered with apprehension. We knew we were going to be moving with the invasion convoys. Ours was the second convoy. The Navy assault ships and landing assault forces made up the first convoy. We were to hit the beach after the combat troops had taken some areas inland. At the last minute, 50 of us were transferred to LST 706 and 50 men from the 391st Night Fighter Squadron were transferred to LST 927. In the event that the main ship with the equipment was lost, there would be some men left to restart the squadron.

On 706, the food was strictly Army—canned or dehydrated. There was room for about 260 men along with bunks or hammocks in the steamy area below deck. I chose to put my cot on deck between a jeep and a 6x6 truck's bumper. It was at the forward starboard side, near the stairs to the hold below, where some others of the 26th were. I was also about nine feet away from a 20mm anti-aircraft gun. The gun emplacement was surrounded by a low, steel protective wall. A three-foot-high steel armor plate ventilator separated the gunner's wall from my cot. The ventilator, with a fan mounted inside, pushed fresh air to the men bunked below. The vent was only four feet from my head.

Once we were on our way, we relaxed. I worked Smoky on deck every day for practice and for the amusement of our buddies. She ate canned stew and bully beef or whatever else was available. I monitored her food intake and waste, trying not to make any drastic changes in her diet, to keep her as healthy as possible. Her little waste bundles were dropped overboard and her puddles were washed away by the daily rain. No baths available here. Her hair became gummy with salt air and her color was now a reddish-brown from brushing against the rusty chains on deck locking down the vehicles. A big Dalmatian, girded by a life preserver, roamed the ship freely.

One becomes mighty sensitive to the ship's tossing in a typhoon's wake, to the smell of diesel fuel coming from short stacks scattered about the tank deck and to the thumping as the ship's propeller lifted out of the water in a high wave. We could also feel the bow jarring at the root of every wave that slowed down the ship a little with each hit.

Our LST was in the second position of the lead column on the right side of the convoy. The tail end of a typhoon made the seas very rough. The fantail and bow of the ships in front and behind were rotating in the 25-foot waves, making them appear and disappear as the ships waddled side-to-side at 10 knots (the speed of the slowest convoy vessels). A destroyer paced at our side about 1,000 feet away as we moved up the west coast of the South Philippines through the Mindanao Sea, the Sulu Sea and, finally, the South China Sea.

Each day at dawn, the skipper ordered the removal of all the canvas shelters the men had set up. This was to eliminate some of the fire hazards, should the ship be hit during an attack. However, every vehicle was loaded with gasoline. We had constant boat drills and alerts. As we approached Mindoro Island, no canvas coverings were permitted at all. Apparently word had been passed that the convoy in front of us had been hit by kamikaze planes.

Generally, a kamikaze pilot was trained only enough to be able to take off in his plane. He was not expected to land. His mission was to strike the enemy with his explosive-loaded aircraft, remaining in it to guide it into the target. Suicide, in the destruction of the enemy, was considered a most honorable way to die. The plane itself was usually a simply-constructed model with few instruments. Sometimes they flew obsolete or damaged aircraft.

Near sundown, just off the coast of Mindoro, four of us were playing cards on a couple of cots, when the first general quarters was sounded. Our drills paid off. Gunners raced to their stations, thrusting on helmets and sliding into life jackets as they ran. The Army men had been wearing the jackets throughout the voyage.

In the distance, to starboard of the convoy, I saw a flight of eight planes backgrounded by a gray, cloudy sky. The ship's loudspeaker ordered Army personnel below deck. Down there, a sailor ran through closing the bulkhead hatches between the compartments. We were warned by the Navy that it was a court-martial offense to open the hatches after they had been closed for general quarters. If a ship was hit, those in a damaged compartment might be lost, but the ship would stay afloat. When the all-clear sounded, I decided I would rather know what was going on, so I took my chances topside.

Dom D'Anglo, Jim Everett, Don Esmond and I continued the pinochle game. About five minutes later, the general quarters horns and bells blared and clanged again, and this time it was for real. I grabbed Smoky, ran to my cot between the jeep and the truck and hit the deck. I pulled the dog close to my ribs and cupped my right hand over her ears. The whole ship began bouncing and vibrating as we opened fire. Twin Bofores (40mm) on the bow were hammering away, as were the two single 40mm guns on each side of the bow. The noise was deafening. The 20mm gunner and his loader were only nine feet away.

Suddenly there was a loud cheer amid the firing! A few moments later, it quieted down, so I gathered up my shaking dog and crawled around on my knees. My hand landed on some of the many small, jagged, silvery cubes on the deck next to me. Standing up now, with Smoky still under my arm and my right hand clamped over her ears I had a clear view of two kamikazes bearing down from two o'clock high, diving at a steep angle across our guns which were aiming and firing at the planes.

The sky was blackened by bursts of flak and everyone around me was standing and yelling, "Come on, get those bastards!" as if this was a football game. The first plane fluttered down into the water next to the bow of the ship directly behind us, sending up a geyser of sea water. The second plane hit a Liberty ship in the second column to our port side. The suicide pilot hit amidship and his target was belching black smoke.

As things quieted down briefly, I noticed the two young Navy gunners on the single 40mm gun just forward of our 20mm. The one on the right was chewing gum as he slowly turned his crank in a backward motion to the rhythm of his gum cracks. The one on the left was moving his crank in a forward motion as the gun moved downward and at the same time to the right.

About a mile out, at 20 feet altitude a plane was heading toward us, straight on the gun position. It kept coming and suddenly, when in was only 500 yards out, KABOOM! KABOOM! KABOOM! Three rounds were fired. The Japanese plane half spiraled sideways, making a big splash in the sea, to another rousing cheer.

The all-clear sounded. The stricken Liberty ship behind us dropped back five ships behind its original position. Black smoke continued to billow up into the sky, trailing behind her.

Dom D'Anglo showed me his bleeding hand. A piece of shrapnel had hit his finger. Norman Smith was lying on the deck with someone leaning over him and someone else calling for medics. Jim Everett and Fred J. Birk, Jr. had been hit, along with four men from the 391st. The only casualties were in our part of the ship located no further than 10 feet away and surrounding us. Smith had a side puncture and needed A-negative blood for a transfusion. The call went out over the loudspeaker. Oscar Feigeles from the photo lab volunteered. He told us later that during the direct transfusion, the needle had popped out and he was pretty upset to see his blood pouring uselessly on the floor.

Smith, whose lung was punctured, was taken off in a landing barge while the convoy was still heading toward Luzon. Ironically, Smith had been the one who never saw the point in digging foxholes. His philosophy was, "If it's going to happen, it's going to happen."

In assessing the damage, we determined that the ship at our port side had been firing at the kamikazes as they passed. A 20mm shell must have fallen short, hitting the inside of the armor-plated fan housing. We found the impact mark, a large dent with scraped-off paint.

Apparently, the shell struck during the first pass of the diving planes, when I was lying down next to the jeep. The shell passed about three feet over my head and hit the ventilator four feet away. Those of us who ducked down were not hit, but those standing were. Most of the shell particles remained inside the ventilator housing while the remaining bouncing-out shrapnel caused the damage. If the shell had hit two inches higher, the gunner would have been struck in the back. Two inches lower would have finished Smoky and me as well as all the men around us. The small metal cubes I had found near me on deck were shell fragments. I knew I had dodged the bullet the tailgunner said I was being saved for.

At twilight, with relative calm settling in, our destroyer escort had dropped back behind us, and I decided to wander aft with Smoky on her leash, looking for a change of scenery. Smoky's salt-gummed hair wafted in clumps in the stormy sea air. I noticed some .50-caliber machine guns being set up and the five-inch gun riding over the ship's propeller. This was a new perspective of the ocean and the convoy.

Things remained peaceful for a time, but the destroyer gunners still maintained their positions. Then, out of nowhere, an airplane appeared, landing lights on, flaps and wheels down, gliding in toward the aft end of the destroyer. The crew of the destroyer appeared mesmerized as it came in on them. The infantrymen on our ship jumped to the machine guns they had set up and opened fire. The gunners of the surrounding ships sent up salvos of 40mm and 20mm shells. The suicide plane was just over the top of the destroyer, with the crew still frozen, looking up at him. Suddenly, the kamikaze reeled from the hits it had taken, peeled over on its side and slammed into the sea sending up a geyser alongside the destroyer. Once again, the witnesses to the episode exploded into wild cheers.

Although general quarters had not been sounded, the ship sent out the all clear signal. The Japanese pilot had attacked in near darkness, confusing the destroyer crew with its flashing lights and lowered landing gear, and had almost succeeded in its goal to hit the ship. For that day's battles, the convoy commander credited LST 706 with the destruction of two enemy planes, but we were sure that we had knocked down three. Even so, when the announcement was made, we all gave one last rousing, "YEEAAAHHHH!"

One of the many unusual actions taken during the heat of battle was the choice of refuge made by John Mordus. He climbed down the anchor chain hole and stood on the anchor, hanging on to the huge chain links. He told us that, if a plane hit us, he planned to let go and jump into the ocean. In reality, the 125-pound Mordus ("Rigger" Mordus to his mates) would likely have been swept under the ship, with disastrous consequences. Later we learned many were killed on the Liberty ship when the kamikaze hit in the center of the ship behind us.

We were indeed lucky. The first assault force, two days ahead of us, took the brunt of 200 attacking suicide planes. Two battleships, the New Mexico and the California, were damaged. In all, 24 ships were sunk and 67 damaged. The kamikaze success rate was almost 50 percent, with some ships taking more than one hit. On the New Mexico, a kamikaze hit the bridge, killing Rear Admiral Theodore Chandler, British Lieutenant General Herbert Lumsden and war correspondent Bill Chickering. A number of others were wounded.

The heavily armed convoy had greatly reduced the number of enemy planes, and only the few remaining ones could be mustered for the attack against our ships. Our convoy lacked the fire power to protect the large number of invasion troops with it, and the all-out defensive firepower raised by the first convoy had given us a real break.

This was by far the largest Naval Force ever gathered in history of warfare. In addition 175,000 troops involved here were ships more than those employed in North Africa, southern France and Italy. Two armies, ten divisions and five regimental combat teams were included. The 26th Photo was the only reconnaissance squadron among the many support units.

Our voyage was less eventful after the convoy cleared Mindoro, but we would never forget the battles of the Mindoro Sea. Before long, we became part of the huge armada anchored in Lingayen Gulf, awaiting orders to hit the beaches. We were supposed to have top-priority landing orders. Instead, we waited for two days, hidden by periodic smoke screens. The dense clouds of white smoke hid our ships from air attack and the strategy worked well. Not only did this mist screen us from the enemy, it screened us off from each other as well. When we could see, we used binoculars to study the neighboring ships, the shoreline and the villages beyond.

The Japanese used another strategy to damage the ships. They floated under wooden boxes and attached high explosives to the sterns of ships waiting to unload. With our carbines, we were put on guard duty with orders to shoot at anything that moved in the water around us. Throughout the nights, the popping of rifles fired at objects, real or imagined, reminded us of the seriousness of our mission. No one got much sleep.

Our assignment on Luzon would put us directly under the Sixth Army instead of the Fifth Air Force. General Krueger, commander of the Sixth Army, was very annoyed our squadron wasn't in operation. In the middle of the night, we got the order, "Hit the beach!" By that time, our troops were holding territory 20 miles along the beach and 10 miles inland. They had faced little resistance because General Yamashita had not expected our troops to land where they did. He used the mountainous areas of Luzon to make his stands. These later battles proved more costly to the U.S.

Before daylight, LST 706 slammed into shore in rough seas. The bow doors opened, the ramp dropped and, barracks bag over my shoulder, carbine in one hand and Smoky and my cot under the other arm, I waded out into the waist-deep water. It was some 40 feet to the beach, where a couple of portable pole lights had been planted in the sand. Other LSTs came in next, some bumping into one another.

There was a stockpile of food nearby and, as we waited for orders, I opened a can of peaches with my hunting knife. Not knowing when we would find food again, I stowed some cans of meat and peaches for Smoky and me. When the tide lowered and the water depth had dropped to one foot, we unfastened the trucks and jeeps from the deck and began to drive them down the steep ramp. Suddenly, the red alert sounded. I grabbed Smoky and we took cover in the darkness behind the pole lights. About a mile down the beach, a direct hit on an ammunition dump sent up fire and smoke that lit the distant sky.

The personnel and equipment needed at the new squadron area were loaded on trucks and quickly driven to the site. The rest of the equipment was unloaded onto the beach with all possible haste. The empty LSTs were moved out of the way to make room for the rest of the ships to unload. In New Guinea we had worked bare-waisted, but here we wore field jackets.

CHAPTER 6

SMOKY STRINGS TELEPHONE WIRES

When the squadron trucks returned, they were quickly loaded and sent back. We were working feverishly to construct the E2 building so the photo lab would be up and running as soon as possible. I hitched a ride on top of the load in a 6x6. The truck climbed off the beach and onto a hard surface road and we rolled past the little town, or barrio, of Dagupan.

Naval shell damage was evident everywhere, particularly on churches, steeples and other stone buildings. Some of the people waved at us as we rode by, others just went about the business of cleaning up the debris. We passed a prisoner of war compound, a hastily built wire enclosure with three somber looking Japanese soldiers inside. Several times we pulled over to allow the hefty tanks to pass.

We drove on, passing rice paddies and nipa houses, and finally arriving in Lingayen, the provincial capital, some 80 miles northwest of Manila. One main street crossed the town, leading to an airstrip. The business section of the town included a Catholic church and a couple of slightly damaged masonry buildings. Combat engineers in bulldozers were busy on the airstrip and trucks were speeding in and out in all directions. The engineers were laying down steel matting, which would eventually cover the runway and its taxiway.

About a mile from the strip, the 26th Photo had taken over a full city block. Nearby, the 391st Night Fighter Group bedded down. At first, we moved into a native nipa house. The thought was that we could get right down to business by saving the time it takes to set up our tents. The Filipinos were asked to vacate every other house and we moved into these bamboo, hemp-tied structures. They were roofed and sided with strips of nipa palm leaves, layered to shed the rain efficiently. There were no window panes, but a sliding nipa panel often filled the gap.

I climbed the three-rung bamboo ladder to enter barren rooms with little sunlight. The floor was made of half-inch wide bamboo, with half-inch wide spaces between each slat. These gaps afforded us the unwelcome sights and smells of the chickens down below. Some of the houses had pigpens underneath. No one wanted to go down to retrieve items that slipped through the cracks. My primary concern was to make sure Smoky's nickel-sized feet didn't slip through the cracks, so I placed a flat board under my cot to enable her to maneuver with less difficulty.

The distant air raids continued during the night and we were awakened in the morning by heavy tanks clattering by on the road next to our shacks. Dust was flying about and we inhaled the stuff long after they passed. The lead tank commander stood out of his hatch, bare-headed and puffing on a big cigar. He assured us that we were still winning.

We continued to set up our base in Lingayen. The natives there were starving. The Japanese had come through periodically, taking whatever pigs, chicken and rice they could appropriate. The situation was desperate, with so many obviously suffering from malnutrition.

The garbage pit was dug for us by some Filipinos, but they stayed around after completing their job, hoping for scraps from our mess kits. Some were scooping up food that had been thrown into the dump. It was a pathetic sight.

A local economy no longer existed. The paper Japanese invasion pesos were worthless. The people were put to work to pump some real money into the economy. Large work groups were organized to take care of squadron duties previously assigned to the GIs. They were permitted to wash pots and pans and to haul cases of food, but not to handle open food. Dr. Pollack had determined that the locals were infested with intestinal parasites.

Many of us hired house boys or girls to clean our tents, sweeping and smoothing the sand floors. Yes, we were back in our tents because Dr. Pollack had decreed the nipa houses unfit for us to live in. We traded food and money for these tasks, and the workers were grateful. We felt good, too. Sometimes they traded gamecocks for our new American pesos. Life was different now, both for them and for us. Until now, we had done our manual labor ourselves. We appreciated the change. The Filipinos had been brutalized by the enemy. Now they were welcome to join us, in work and in recreation. We became good neighbors immediately.

The local mothers, in true Spanish tradition, accompanied their daughters as chaperons to the nightly movies. These dignified women, proudly ignoring the poverty surrounding them, came in their finest linen and lace, and their beautiful butterfly-sleeved dresses added a touch of elegance to our evenings. The army paid rent for any buildings they used and many of the men were skilled craftsmen who assisted our carpenters and painters.

One local pest, the sand flea, was all too plentiful. Smoky needed daily baths in my helmet. But she was happy here, and slept contentedly under the mosquito netting at the foot of my cot.

F-5s were soon flying recon missions off the steel-matted runways, first to nearby targets. Then, as the infantry moved along to Baguio and dark Field, they flew to those tough resistance areas.

My new tent companions were Alan Kuzmicki, a camera repairman and former art instructor at the University of Georgia; John Barnard, a photo lab technician and art student from California; John Graham, a squadron mail clerk from Michigan; and Jack Tankersly, a lab technician from Oklahoma. Our first task was to dig a bomb shelter in the soft sand. It was large enough for all of us and was covered over by coconut palm logs and nipa leaves, which held the foot of sand we piled on top.

One night, our letter writing was interrupted by the usual red alert and we headed for the shelter. In the darkness we were about bowled over by someone trying to get inside before us. The freshly lit candlelight revealed a grinning Norm Smith, the guy who didn't believe in foxholes. After being so seriously wounded in the kamikaze attack, he had become a believer and gladly joined us in the shelter as the bombs were dropping at the airstrip.

Smoky was beginning to react nervously to the explosions. As soon as she heard them in the distance she began to spin in circles. A dog's hearing is more sensitive than ours and I was not surprised that these violent noises would produce fear in her. Every time we were under attack, I cupped my hands over her ears until the all clear sounded.

An Army major, directly assigned to us, flew a Piper Cub back and forth to the front lines and to headquarters with our aerial photos, as soon as they were dry. The sets of prints were distributed to MacArthur's command post and to his field generals. Admiral Nimitz and his fleet commanders also received the daily aerial photos. We could feel it! We were part of something big!

While waiting for the photos one day, the major and I struck up a conversation about pet dogs. He had been watching Smoky play tug-of-war with the guys in the finishing room. As we chatted about our four-legged friends, he told me he loved to hunt waterfowl on Chesapeake Bay with his wonderful retriever. He remembered the day he had taken his big dog out when the wind was high and the water was rough. He had flushed out a flock of ducks and downed one with a shotgun blast. His eager partner leaped into the surf for the retrieve. The bird was being carried out by the wind-driven waves and the dog was struggling to reach it.

As his master watched from shore, the dog tried valiantly to make headway against the surf and finally disappeared from view. The major said he faced the sad realization that he had lost his faithful friend. He waited there for more than an hour before he gave up and sadly returned to his home several miles away. Seven hours later, he heard a noise outside his door and opened it to find his great Chesapeake Bay Retriever wagging his tail and holding the duck between his softly closed jaws. It was a wonderful story about a fine breed.

One sunny afternoon, I had a visitor from the Communications Section. Sgt. Bob Gapp eyed Smoky with curiosity, hemmed and hawed a bit and finally, in an embarrassed manner, explained his purpose in coming to see us.

"Say, Bill," he began somewhat sheepishly, "we have a problem down at the airstrip. We have to get our telephone lines through an eight-inch-wide drainage culvert that runs 60 feet under the taxiway. I saw a newsreel where a cat did that in Alaska. They fastened a string to the cat's collar, blocked him in the pipe so he couldn't back out and frightened him through with a loud burst of compressed air."

He looked at me sympathetically and continued, "But it seems Smoky is a very smart dog and maybe we could coax her through the pipe." If she could do it, he knew it would save days of work removing the steel matting, digging up the culvert, putting in the wire and then reversing the whole process. Meanwhile, during the operation, all aircraft parking traffic would have to be diverted to a distant field.

"Can you see daylight through the pipe?" I asked.

"Yes, in the upper part," he replied.

"The only way we'll try it," I warned, "is that, if she gets stuck, your gang will dig her out by going down from the top of her location."

"Of course, we'll be happy to!" Gapp agreed wholeheartedly.

We hopped into his weapons' carrier and set off for the line. Gapp suggested that we could tie a string to Smoky's collar. The string was extremely lightweight and could be easily broken if it caught on something in inside the pipe, allowing her to escape.

At the airstrip, three culverts lay side by side, each boxed in by a wooden frame. I looked into the center one and saw daylight at the other end. The others had very little light showing. These culverts were constructed with short sections of corrugated, semi-rounded, galvanized steel pushed together with some overlapping. At the section joints, some five feet apart, sand had sifted down into the pipes. These sand piles were at each intersection, leaving only three or four inches of clearance in the pipes.

"You promise we'll dig her out if we have to?" I asked. I wanted to make sure our agreement was understood.

"Absolutely!" Gapp assured me.

"Then, here's what we'll do." I said. "Bob, you hold Smoky at the opening. I'll go over to the other side of the strip, and when you're ready, I'll call her through the pipe."

Just then a P-51 Mustang, one of our brand-new fighter planes, taxied across the steel matting over the culvert. The sound was deafening! It sounded like steel thimbles being dragged over a metal washboard-only magnified a thousand times!

"We'll wait until it quiets down," Gapp suggested.

Several of our P-38s on the parking pads nearby were being revved up by their mechanics. We tied the string to Smoky's collar. Gapp's assistant unwound the long string and measured it over the runway to the full length of the pipe. We all wanted to make sure the string was long enough to be pulled by the dog through the pipe, with plenty to spare.

At last, the area quieted down. No planes were coming to the taxiway and the mechanics had finished their engine work. We were ready to go. I yelled, "All set!"

"Okay, she's in place," Gapp yelled back.

"Come, Smoky, come!" I ordered. I was lying on my belly, peering through the pipe. I could see her head silhouetted against the light. She hesitated and started to turn back.

"Come, Smoky, come!" I ordered her again.

"Is she still coming?" I called out.

"Ya, I'm still feeding line!" Gapp shouted.

Suddenly Gapp warned, "She's caught!"

"Smoky! Stand, stay!" I commanded.

She turned and looked at Gapp, as if to say, "What's holding us up here?" Gapp wiggled the line. "Okay, she's free!"

"Come, Smoky, come! Come on, baby, come on!" I encouraged "Is she still coming?"

"Ya, I'm still feeding line," the excited lineman assured me. By this time, the dust from her movement was blocking the view. I was still encouraging her to come, when I spotted those two amber eyes about 15 feet away from me.

"Atta girl, atta girl!" I shouted, "She's here!"

She broke into a run and flew into my outstretched arms. Gapp was laughing as he hurried over, pulled a few more feet of line through and cut Smoky loose. The Yorkie was as pleased as we were. "Boy, Smoky deserves a big steak," Gapp proclaimed. "I'm heading for the mess hall to get her one." A big steak for a four-pound dog is about the size of a mini burger, but she had earned her reward. Her task may have taken only a few minutes, but it was a breathtaking, sweaty few minutes.

Back at the squadron, the news spread fast. Smoky was famous once again. In no time at all, the signal section had three thick cables strung through the culvert.

From the moment she pulled the string through the pipe under the taxi strip, in the combat area of Lingayen Gulf resulting in teletype and phone lines being made available for communications to the combat squadrons on the airfield, she moved from mascot category to WAR DOG. This was not a gimmick, because telephone poles with wires could be not erected near the small combat air field. The only way to get wires laid was by placing them in a drainage ditch over a mile long to the other side of the 60' long 8" diameter culvert under the steel matted taxi strip-road then following the ditch to the maintenance buildings.

Only seven inches tall at the shoulder. Smoky was a logical solution to the problem to taking the alternative of tearing up the strip to lay the wires, force the planes to be parked out parallel to the runway in a line exposed to enemy bombing. (The 5th Air Force destroyed 300 Japanese planes on the ground parked this way at Hollandia in April'44.) Our planes were parked in small groups so a bomb would have to be pinpointed to hit a couple of planes. The digging up, laying the wires and replacing the strip would have taken several days. The actual going through the pipe took less than two minutes. She was untrained for the task but trusted me so much that she came through although she was lost from sight most of the way.

Smoky knew she accomplished something special responding to our enthusiasm by jumping with joy, her whole back end wagging furiously as she struck my ankles with her forepaws. Other than the personal thrill of her achievement we didn't think that much of it at the time. (Some WAR DOGS were trained to crawl while laying wire from a reel mounted on their backs.) When the editor of "WING DING" (the 91st Photo Wing

Headquarters which printed newsletters sent to all Squadrons) heard about it, he asked for a story and a photo. This was reenacted for the article. It took time to appear because the Wing Headquarters was on the Philippine Island of Mindoro and thus resulting in slow correspondence lags as we were at the advanced base on Luzon.

In dog training, it is important for a rapport to be maintained by constant companionship. A dog and master are always being molded into a team, each learning about the habits of the other and what is expected of the other. The more they are together the better the team becomes. Although it is good for dogs to be around other people and to be petted and held by them, the relationship with its master is all-important. Smoky went to the movies every night and everyone wanted to hold her. She was good company for all, but I never let anyone try to make her do her tricks. That would have wrecked the discipline and teamwork we had established and might have confused her. Still, she was a regular, all-around dog and she enjoyed all the attention.

As time went on, the raids were fewer and of little significance. New sound movies were shown in the squadron center every night and we also watched newsreels reporting the war's progress. We built a bamboo stage with a floor made of flat boards. Nipa palm leaves provided protective cover and homemade, conical-shaped tin stage lights completed our little theater.

During the evening shows, we often saw a rat climb a coconut tree and walk out on the phone wire about 10 feet above our outdoor movie area. The wire was strung between the projector and the movie screen and fastened to two trees. Each time the rat was at midpoint on the wire, his shadow projected on the screen and he was spotlighted by the flickering movie light. He'd stop and sit there with his tail waving back and forth to keep his balance, watch the movie, then move on a few minutes later to the other tree. A little later, he'd come back and repeat his performance. One night someone climbed the tree while our visitor was doing his thing, pulled down the wire and let it go like a bowstring. Up the movie screen the shadow flew and then down again with a thud. The rat never returned.

The war raged on and the 26th continued to meet the requests of the vast combined armies spreading over Luzon. Many bitter battles were fought for this island. Some of our pilots returned to the States, others stayed on and a number of our young men lost their lives in this intense effort to regain the Philippines.

Lt. Karl N. Booth, who had been with the squadron from its beginning, failed to return from a low-level, 500 foot altitude, morning mission to Ipo Dam. Ipo Dam was important for the U.S. to capture before the foe could destroy its Manila water supply. CO. Major Gathers personally searched for Booth in that afternoon. No luck.

Lt. Madison Gillesby begged Gathers for permission to look for the extremely popular Booth. Gillesby failed to return. Gathers searched for both men to no avail. Gathers felt particularly bad as both men should have returned to the States long before. Later, their planes were found crashed close together, downed by enemy artillery guns hidden in the hillside. Lt. Clarence Cook died on another mission and was buried by natives. Former squadron member Lt. John S. Dunaway, an Ace with 7 planes to his credit, crashed into the sea.

In spite of these sad reminders of the seriousness of the conflict, we pressed on. One way to take one's mind off the reality of war was usually after supper when Smoky and I walked away from the compound, enjoying the balmy evenings. These quiet moments offered me the opportunity to reflect on our experiences. The palm-shaded streets and lovely beaches were a peaceful sanctuary away from the turmoil of our work. As we headed for the ocean, we watched people tending their livestock. In the rice paddies, men and women knee-deep in water waved to us as we passed. Some evenings we might see a small boy on a water buffalo, using a stick to urge his mount to pull the plow and break the ground.

Smoky had given up chasing chickens. On one of our jaunts, she enraged a mother hen by bothering the chicks and the hen jumped all over the little dog. Now she gave a wide berth to all chicken families. But-gamecocks, look out! We often practiced our routines when we were alone on the beach. The spectacular sunsets and sparkling water are pleasant images forever etched on my brain.

The native people were of a peaceful disposition and spoke a very understandable, broken English along with a native tongue that was one of 88 different dialects spoken in the Philippine Islands. The men were skilled in woodworking and the women in sewing, embroidering and fancy stitching. I employed a local lady's talents to add to the embroidery on Smoky's coat blanket. We added "SMOKY Champion Yank Mascot SWPA 1944." She also stitched on a blank patch for past and future assignments and travel and rearranged the other insignia.

Next, I located a carpenter and asked him to build a sliding board for Smoky. It was to be eight feet long with sides, six inches apart, and the upright boards four inches high. We also needed a platform and a ladder to enable the dog to climb up to it I asked how much the completed job would cost. He grinned at me and said he didn't want any money, just a camera.

Just a camera! In these remote areas, a camera was almost impossible to find. Anyone who had one refused to part with it. I had bought a Leica on Biak for 10 dollars. It had come in a cigar box, totally disassembled. I carried around that jumble of tiny screws, nuts, bolts, springs and cloth curtains, but with no service manual to guide me, I couldn't do anything with it. Someone who claimed to be a camera expert bought it from me for 15 dollars. I did have a simple box camera, film size 127, with a small plug-in flash attachment. It was quite primitive, but when I showed it to the carpenter, he said he was happy with the barter. I showed him how to load and unload it correctly, how to take pictures and advance the film. He was thrilled. Three days later, he astonished me by showing up with the sliding board, ladder and platform crafted of beautiful Philippine mahogany. It was truly a work of art.

Our squadron painter, Henri Wickham, did a great job, too. He painted it circus red with white bars. He also painted the squadron insignia on the barrel Smoky used in one of her tricks. The insignia featured Donald Duck, sporting a red helmet and a flying yellow scarf, and shooting from his cloud perch with an aerial camera. Walt Disney had donated the design for our use without restriction.

To complete the wire-walking apparatus I had brought from Biak, I made a wooden stanchion and mounted the rig so it could be moved about intact. The parachute riggers made Smoky a red and white aircrew cap with an extra long peak. The mechanics wore them to keep their hair clean and to shade their eyes from the sun.

Once again the clever seamstress helped me add to Smoky's wardrobe. She fashioned two clown suits from colorful pieces of salvaged parachutes. The zipper on the yellow and green suit had to be the biggest zipper per square inch of material ever used, but it was the only one available. The yellow clown suit had a musical bar and notes stitched in green on the sides. Smoky was ready for show business.

There were pets everywhere on the base. Monkeys were plentiful, puppies even more plentiful and gamecocks the most plentiful of all. Dogs were commonplace in the village of Lingayen. Most were mongrels with inbreeding faults, incapable of the intelligent responses we were used to seeing. Whether pure or cross-bred, our dogs were more alert. The village dogs were stunted, short-haired and, to us, surprisingly alike. (Perhaps they resembled the ancient dogs who came before man began developing hybrids and breeds.) These animals were as malnourished as their owners and, given the hardships of war, it was a wonder that any had survived. The GIs were buying them for five or ten pesos each. (A peso was worth 50 cents American.)

One day a teletype bulletin was posted outside the orderly room. We were stunned by the news of the death of President Franklin D. Roosevelt. Most of us had sent in absentee ballots to reelect him in 1944. I had turned 21 in March and cast my first vote ever for FDR. Margie wrote that he had not looked well in pictures taken before the election. He kept out of the public eye and had done no campaigning. She was not surprised by his death. Now Harry Truman was Commander-in-Chief and we were all certain he would carry on well and end the war.

During a casual conversation one day, I remarked, "Holy Christmas!" Smoky jumped up and down. Surprised, I repeated, "Christmas!" She jumped around enthusiastically. Did this little tyke understand Christmas?

"Sport!" I shouted, and she was all excited again.

"Rover!" The same reaction. So much for that.

But this dog was so exceptionally clever, she might have understood. If she was loose and thirsty, she would saunter over to the bag of drinking water near the center of the squadron area, and get the attention of the first guy passing by. She simply ran up to the bag and barked, then ran to the man and barked, then ran back to the bag and barked until the GI got the message.

Gathering water in his cupped hands, he would let her lap it up until she was full. The guys got a kick out of it. At times, when she was trying to locate me, she sniffed everyone's ankles, dashing around among their feet, never looking up, until she sniffed me and celebrated by bounding around her master's legs. It became a hide-and-seek game she played with me. If Smoky wanted to get away alone to do some exploring, she would circle in a little path around me, making sure I was engrossed in conversation, and then, when the little path took her behind me, she would slip away. Eventually, as I grew wise to this ploy, she started making wider and wider circles around me. She kept her nose to the ground, pretending to be exploring, but, as she circled she cast quick glances at me without moving her head to see if she was being watched. If it seemed to her that I was not looking, she'd scoot away. Then I'd yell, "Stand! Stay!" freezing her in her tracks, and recall her with, "Smoky, come!" A smart dog is thinking all the time and it was a real challenge for me to stay ahead of Smoky.

Her obedience training actually saved her life on one occasion. We were out for a walk when she spotted another dog across a heavily traveled road and, without looking, she dashed toward him. One of our ten-wheeler trucks was thundering past and I shouted, "STAND! STAY!" in my loudest voice. She froze and the truck's wheels clattered by, just six inches from her tiny nose. That was a close one!

If I planned to continue our intense training program, I would need a house to work in. The tents and houses were so close together that we had little ground space for practicing her tricks. I asked 1st Sgt. J.B. Howell to inspect the house next to my tent, hoping he would give me permission to use it. He crawled up the ladder, looked around and said, "Absolutely. Go right ahead. If you need anything else, let me know."

Lab chief Green donated the lumber to cover the bamboo floor. A couple of 16x20 cardboard boxes, bent in half, made excellent little hurdles. Windham stenciled the Hawkeye group insignia on them, using the same stencil he used for the planes.

The plywood flooring was perfect for our equipment. Here we could use the scooter, the sliding board, the rolling drum and the tight-wire rig. I even had her jumping through a bamboo hoop we had taken from a small fish net. We were really polishing our act. I thought maybe I could teach her to spell her name. In this quiet atmosphere, I decided to give it a try.

I had never seen this trick done before, so we were breaking new ground. Smokey seemed to be a more conventional spelling of her name, and many published stories about Smoky spelled with the e. I didn't want her to have to learn six letters, though. The first letters I used were 14 inches high, SMOKY, cut from cardboard photo paper boxes. I braced them with sturdy strips glued to the backs, so that they would stand up.

I wanted to impress the letter forms on her mind, so I carried her over to the letter S, held her head and traced the S shape with her face, over and over, while saying "S" out loud. The next day, I repeated the process with the letter M, and then went over the S and the M. The third day, it was 0. This time I not only traced the 0, but put her head inside the circle as well. Each day, I tried to teach her a new letter as well as going over them all in sequence. We practiced repeatedly. She didn't get it.

After three weeks, I tried mixing up the letters but also continued trying them in order. By now, I was saying, "Smoky, spell your name," calling out S, M, 0, K, Y. I had her standing in front of the letters while I stood behind, facing her. It was hard work. I tried teaching her early in the morning, before the 100-degree heat set in. Rainy days were ideal because the air was cool and the flights were grounded. Two months passed and Smoky was still at square one. We gave up on "Spell Your Name."

The squadron area was suddenly plagued with a disease that caused chickens to keel over instantly and many dogs to fall sick and die in a matter of days. As soon as I got wind of it, I isolated Smoky from other animals. Early one morning, as I worked my shift in the lab, I noticed a couple of figures, about 50 feet away, digging in the sand. It was 3:00 a.m., a very odd time to be digging, so I investigated. There, lying lifeless on the sand, was Smoky's six-month-old pup, Topper. He had died during the night and Frank Petrilak and Howard Kalt were burying him. The scourge was quick and deadly. Within 10 days there were only four surviving dogs in our squadron, a newly arrived Irish setter, a very ill pup, Duke and Smoky.

Smoky's old pal Colonel Turbo, mascot of the 25th Photo, had met his doom as well. A member of the 25th told me that the monkey had become even more vicious and had badly bitten his keeper. His destructiveness had increased to the extent that some of his severest critics had formed a firing squad. Turbo was read his service record and his orders and then dispatched, 1,2,3, FIRE! He had no survival skills for the jungle and was too destructive and dangerous to live around people, so like the old army song, the story is probably true, "Old soldiers never die they just fade away."

In April, Warrant Officer Mosket of camera repair approached me at the photo lab. He wanted to confirm my ability to install aerial cameras. He asked if I would mind a transfer to his outfit. I was no longer flying combat missions and, since I knew everyone over there and the job was always daywork, I agreed to transfer. The battle over dark Field had long been under way and Manila had been taken with a terrible loss of lives, mostly among the Filipinos. On February 5, 1945, a 1st Cavalry American tank pulled up to the Santo Tomas internment camp, blasted off the front gates and liberated the 3,521 prisoners of war, mostly Americans. These were the first Americans to arrive in Manila. The war in the Pacific was going well.

Special Service was planning a variety show with a Filipino and GI cast. I was asked to be a part of it. I hesitated at first, but then agreed. A musical accompaniment was arranged to match what Smoky and I were planning as a routine. Henry Shacklette, the Camera Repair electrician would play the Solovox he took everywhere with him. A Solovox was an electric keyboard that attached to a piano to add sounds. We began with "Through the Legs" to the tune of "Pretty Baby." Then we did "Dead Dog" with the "Funeral March." As Smoky jumped over the hurdles, our musician switched to "Oh Where Oh Where Has My Little Dog Gone." "Beer Barrel Polka" accompanied the "Barrel Walk" and the "Scooter" music was "My Merry Oldsmobile." For her big finish, "The Daring Young Man on the Flying Trapeze" played as she climbed the ladder and walked the tightwire from one platform to the other. Then I covered her eyes with the kerchief and she moved cautiously over the wire to the first platform. When the blindfold was removed, she sailed down the sliding board.

We used this exact routine every time afterward.

But not this time. I chickened out. I told them the dog wasn't ready, but it was me! I wasn't ready. I thought about all those guys sitting out front and I just couldn't face it. I was not a professional and had never performed before an audience, except at the hospital, where those watching numbered no more than 20 or 30. But here it would be before the whole squadron! The director was really mad and told me to go to hell. I was shaken. The next day, I recovered my courage and went back to him to volunteer once more. He said, "No! You had your chance and blew it. That's final!"

It was final. Through the years it always bothered me that most of the squadron never got to see Smoky perform. Oh, they saw bits and pieces of the routine on ship decks or in the squadron area or in the photo lab. But they never saw the whole act, and I would always regret that.

A letter came from Barbara Wood Smith asking me if I would bring Smoky to Manila. Santo Tomas University, the former site of the prison camp, had now become a General Army Hospital and she wanted us to perform there.

Smoky and I boarded a truck and went directly to Santo Tomas. We performed in 15 wards and received the same wonderful response that we had been given in the past. We used very little equipment. I gave a quick demonstration of obedience, explaining how each exercise is used in dog shows. I knew a bit about this from my classes in Cleveland.

Of course we did the walking through the legs ("grapevine") and a little Jitterbug. For this dance we faced each other, each lifting the opposite foot four times, and then spun around in opposite directions, coming back face to face. We got plenty of laughs with that one. Playing dead and singing finished up our 10- to 15-minute routine. We were always asked, "How did Smoky get to New Guinea?" It was still a question I could not answer. Smoky's singing was always a howling success. One GI patient asked if he could take her to sing in the other wards. A lady photographer from the Red Cross took pictures of us with the soldiers. Later, we set Smoky out on the lawn in a helmet, a C-ration box and GI shoes. It was a lot like the Yank photo but Smoky's tongue was hanging out from the heat and I couldn't get her to pull it in. She looked like a dog-tired soldier.

Barbara wanted to know if we would like to be on the Red Cross weekly radio broadcast back to the States. I thought that would be great! We drove off in a jeep to downtown Manila where the Red Cross had its headquarters and where The Mutual News Network was located. We were taken into a sound room where a new device called wire recording was being used for our interview. Instead of rotating a 78-rpm disk, they used a silvery wire moving from reel to reel. That was, of course, the predecessor of plastic tape recording.

The interviewer, Sue Tate, spoke with a marvelous southern accent. She began, "This is Sue Tate of the American Red Cross in Manila." Then she asked me questions about Smoky's status as Champion Yank Mascot of the SWPA and about her stringing the wire under the airstrip. Then she told her radio audience about Bill Wynne and Smoky giving performances in the service hospitals. The interview lasted about three minutes. It was to be broadcast, on a given date, over 100 Mutual stations back in the states.

I notified Margie and my mother, and they had 78-rpm records of the broadcast cut by WHK, the Mutual Network station in Cleveland. About the same time, Acme News Pictures released the Red Cross photo of Smoky in the helmet and describing her as an entertainer in GI hospitals. One Sunday newspaper clipping showed her side-by-side with Chips, a cross German Shepherd, who had been awarded the Silver Star for heroism and the Purple Heart. (The Army took the medals away later, when it decided that animals should not receive such honors.) Several squadron members received letters and newspaper clippings from home. Their families and friends had either heard the broadcast or read about our wonder dog.

Lieutenants Henry R. Willis and James L. Wilson came to the 26th at the same time as young flight officers. They were inseparable. They had come through flight training together and, listed together alphabetically, they had been cut into the 26th together. Their last mission was low level, over Kiangan, Luzon, on July 10, 1945. They were listed as missing in action. Both shot down by enemy anti-aircraft fire, their planes had crashed in a mountain valley. They were found side by side.

There were so many hazards for those serving in the Pacific. Some men died from malaria. Others suffered with jungle rot or dysentery, or were plagued with other jungle diseases or pests. We were attacked by mosquitoes, ants and all manner of creeping things. We couldn't leave even the tiniest amounts of food on the tables because of the swarming ants. Our table legs were placed in cans of water to keep the ants out. We put a spot of motor oil in the water to hold down evaporation and to eliminate the mosquitoes from hatching. Finally, we were issued the first aerosol bombs, which were a real godsend. If we had had them sooner, there would have been far fewer cases of malaria and dengue fever.

Huge centipedes sent two men to the hospital. One was bitten in his bed and Johannes Tietjen, our carpenter, was jolted by one of these hard-shelled villains hiding in his shoe.

Smoky, the little battler, took on a six-inch specimen. She was overconfident in her strategy. She rolled over on her back on top of the centipede and got a nasty sting just above her thigh. Boy, did she yelp! I sweated it out, not knowing what to expect, but, when she had rested a bit, she recovered nicely. The sting killed a patch of hair the size of a silver dollar and turned the skin black. That mark lasted for three years.

The war in Europe had ended, but the fighting on Luzon continued. More than 40,000 Japanese troops were still holding out in the north. According to General Krueger's book, "From Down Under to Nippon," the casualties on Luzon were high. Americans: 8,140 killed in action, 29,557 wounded, 157 missing in action. Japanese: 173,563 killed in action, 7,297 missing in action. There were no stats on the number of Japanese wounded.

Toward the end of July, we were preparing to leave for Okinawa. Captain Mac called a squadron formation to brief us about the move. "We must strip ourselves of many personal possessions," he said, "and no animals will be permitted to go. Except Smoky. She has been with us a long time as squadron mascot and she doesn't take up much space." As it turned out, most guys who had pets took them along anyway.

We gave many of our treasures to our Filipino friends, who watched sadly as we struck our tents and tore down the shelters that had covered some of our equipment. We tried to return their property as we had found it, except for a few improvements. We waved goodbye from the tops of the loaded trucks as we slowly rolled out of the village. We knew we would never see them again.

We loaded onto an old LST #31. Our move to Okinawa was to be involved with the invasion of Japan, so we joined the other ships in Subic Bay to form a convoy and prepared to head out to sea again.

A dark, mysterious American submarine lay next to us and smoke screens once again hid us from view. We put out to sea for Okinawa, past the Ryukus, islands bitterly fought for only a few months before. Our voyage was peaceful, but on Okinawa, 5,000 marines and soldiers died on land and another 5,000 sailors were killed at sea. The relentless kamikazes had done their job. Japan lost 70,000 men here and 80,000 Okinawan civilians lost their lives on their island.

CHAPTER 7

ATOM BOMBS

We could see Ie Shima from where we were stationed on the island. Ernie Pyle, the great war correspondent had been killed there shortly before we arrived. Of the 733 reporters assigned to cover the war, very few had visited our theater of operations. We had no fancy officers' clubs to offset the daily grind. In the Asiatic Pacific, the ground forces' daily fare of poor food seldom attracted classy press coverage. But Pyle had come. It was sadly ironic that the man who was physically exhausted from the effort and travel he had put into his worldwide reporting should die here in our so-called minimum war. We had read his intimate interviews with GIs and we knew he understood us. We were shaken by his death.

The day's work was done and we were waiting in the chow line, when a long, yellow-paper teletype message was tacked on the bulletin board. It announced the bombing of Hiroshima. The news that this bomb, packed with the equivalent of 20,000 tons of TNT, had leveled a city was stunning. Such destructive power was unbelievable. One B-29 Superfortress had dropped a payload that killed 45,000 people. Our reactions ranged from quiet elation at the thought of the war's imminent end to terrible sadness for the people of Hiroshima. The bulletins kept coming in, one every few hours. We learned that the city had been warned to evacuate, through leaflets dropped from our planes. The warning was largely ignored. Japan refused to surrender unconditionally. Two days later, we were shocked to hear that a second bomb had been dropped on Nagasaki.

Then we heard what we had been waiting for—the cessation of hostilities they called it. August 15, 1945 was the date set to officially end World War II. It would be some time, though, before we could go home.

Our Okinawa campsite was still surrounded by the barbed wire the combat troops had strung, and tied to the wire were tin cans full of gravel that would rattle if anyone touched them. The hand grenades we removed from the wire were also a serious reminder of the conflict so recently ended.

The long caves running beside the roads were cleared out and the construction of the photo lab was halted. We did finish the mess hall, though. When the natives saw us nailing the corrugated steel to the roof, they laughed and told us about big winds. Heeding their warning, we topped each corner of the roof sections with large sand bags. The tiny local houses were built of 10-inch-thick stone and mortar and their roofs were made of heavy red tiles. There were no glass windows.

I never volunteered to perform with Smoky because I didn't know where to sign up. In New Guinea, the Army nurses had been the first ones to show off my Yorkie. The Red Cross nurses had urged us to entertain in Australia. On Luzon, the USO had big stars like Joe E. Brown working the hospitals and I thought it might be presumptuous of me to offer our services.

But, here on Okinawa, someone found us and asked us to put on our show at a servicemen's recreation hall run by the Red Cross. We were ready! Henry Shacklette brought his Solovox and Howard Kalt, his magic act. A 6x6 truck carried all our gear and 10 members of the squadron who wanted to see the show.

When our turn came to go on, we hustled the Solovox and our paraphernalia out on stage and waited as Kalt introduced us,

"And now...Corporal Bill Wynne and Corporal Smoky!"

We ran out onto the stage and bounced through our routine exactly as we had rehearsed it. The music was perfect, changing to highlight each trick. As we scurried off stage, Shacklette gave us a final fanfare and the audience roared their approval. Everything had come off without a hitch and we were a big success.

The word was that the Japanese envoys were to land at Ie Shima and that we would be able to see their planes from our campsite. The prospect was exciting and we were all waiting and watching when that day finally came. Prior to this, our biggest thrill had been listening to the radio as General MacArthur had stipulated the terms of the surrender. Several of us stood on the hood of a jeep facing Ie Shima and listened to the air-to-ground radio transmission. Six P-38s were escorting the peace party. We could hear the radio counting down the miles as the planes approached.

The envoys would come in white bombers painted with large green crosses, by order of the U.S. Army. This was the first leg of their journey. From Okinawa they would fly to Manila to board the Battleship Missouri for the actual signing of the peace pact.

We were thrilled to be witnesses of this historic flight. The Japanese pilots were reluctant to identify themselves by the stipulated code. A nervous American voice came over the radio, requesting the verification code, "Bataan I and Bataan II, come in."

"Sorry, cannot hear you, cannot hear you," was the halting Japanese reply.

"Come on, you son of a bitch, or we'll knock you out of the air!" a second American voice demanded.

"I can hear you! I can hear you!" the Japanese voice called out urgently and completed the code with the hated words, "Bataan I and Bataan II," just as the planes came into view. The P-38s were riding herd at four o'clock high.

Someone near me yelled, "It's over! DAMN—IT'S OVER!"

"That it is," I laughed in relief.

The number of lives saved by this early surrender has been estimated at 2,000,000. The allies were planning to land 1,250,000 men in Japan beginning November 2, 1945. Vast numbers of troops were en route from Europe to help the Pacific forces. The Japanese government was arming every man and woman with weapons that ranged from sidearms to pitchforks and pointed wooden spears, expecting their people to fight to the death.

Research shows that the bombs dropped on Hiroshima and Nagasaki took fewer civilian lives than the Japanese had taken on Luzon and Okinawa. At that time more than 52 million people had already died from the effects of World War II. Mankind had reached its pinnacle of destruction in those few years and, with the advent of atomic weapons, a global war would be far too costly, even for the victor. Full-scale warfare had become obsolete.

Although the 26th Photo unit's casualties were among the heaviest of the 5th Air Force Photo Recon squadrons, they were relatively light: 13 dead and 10 wounded or injured. We were fortunate. We were glad it was all over, but none of us would ever forget those we left behind. We didn't know how soon we might be heading home. Although our squadron was assigned to Korea, some were able to go back to the States sooner. Most of the 5th Air Force was going to Japan. Some of us who had dogs volunteered to stay on Okinawa, so we didn't have to face the long days of ocean travel. We would be able to fly to Korea later. Those who stayed behind were attached to 6th Group Headquarters, which provided our meals. We bulldozed most of our photo supplies, but the E2 building, the portable photo lab, was left there.

It was quiet in the two remaining tents we shared. John Hembury was still there with Duke and one other GI had stayed behind with his sickly pup. Smoky developed an infection in her nasal passages, causing constant coughing and sneezing. In just two days it became chronic. She wagged her tail and seemed all right, but I was alarmed by the amount of mucus she was sneezing out.

About a quarter of a mile down the road, the 4th Marine War Dog Platoon was encamped, so I walked there, hoping to find a vet. I was told that a medic was taking care of the dogs. As I approached his tent, I was greeted by the barking of Shepherds and Dobermans, but thankfully, they were all chained to their dog houses. I found the medic corporal sitting at a field desk inside the tent. He said he had no medicine for Smoky's sinus infection but suggested I feed her a mixture of fresh milk and eggs.

He took me outside to introduce me to the war dogs. Pointing to one of the Shepherds he said, "That one saved his patrol twice." One dog was barking furiously.

He gestured toward him and explained, "That's a one-man dog. His master was killed in a fox-hole and the dog wouldn't let anyone near the body. Finally, one of the guys took an ax handle and beat him into submission. He's the only man who can handle him now. The dog was so mean the patrol had to tie him down outside the foxholes. He tackled anybody. But he also alerted us to danger long before the other dogs did."

Some of the other dogs there had been cited for bravery and some were still recovering from their wounds. It was a rare and memorable experience for me.

Back at the mess hall, all I could find were dehydrated milk and powdered eggs. I added a bit of water, mixed them together and let Smoky gulp them down. The next day, her sneezes were less liquid. I fed her the mixture morning, noon and night and in just three days she was well again. I have never found anyone who ever heard of this cure.

There seemed to be no hope for the sick puppy. We were concerned for the safety of the other dogs. We watched helplessly as the little fellow went from bad to worse, with no one able to help him. He suffered with constant fits and the shakes and we were convinced that he must be destroyed. We suggested to Zeitlin, his owner, that the situation was hopeless and offered our help when the time came to end the pup's life. None of us had any experience in this kind of thing, but we decided to dig a hole and tie the dog to stake at the bottom of the hole. Zeitlin shot the pup in the head with his carbine. We were all feeling terrible as we covered over the little grave. Zeitlin was devastated.

For the next few days, we busied ourselves with preparations to face a typhoon that was heading our way. Forecasters warned that we were directly in its path. We used plywood from the photo lab leftovers to make walls protecting two sides of our 20x20 tents. As we nailed these walls to the tent posts, we felt confident that we were ready for the storm.

At 11:00 that night, the typhoon hit. The wind-driven rain battered against our tent walls and they held. We went to sleep reassured and were wakened at 3:00 a.m. by an eerie silence. We sat on our cots discussing this strange calm and then dozed off. At 5:00, we were jolted from our slumber by a great POOOOOFFFFF! — the sound of our tent being blown away. The wind had changed direction and turned our tent into a giant kite.

We were instantly soaked, so we grabbed our blankets and cots, and ran for the mess hall, still standing nearby. My cot was snatched from my grasp with Smoky attached; it rose into the air and, before I caught up to it, turned two cartwheels, spinning Smoky in mid-air. I tackled the cot about 50 feet from the original tent site. Corrugated metal pieces were hurtling through the air like huge whirling knives. Everything I saw was airborne.

With Smoky under my arm, I pointed my cot straight ahead and fought my way to the mess hall. The wind speed was 80 m.p.h., and the worst was yet to come. Once inside the hall, I put the cot against the wall and set Smoky down on it. The torrential rain was blowing through the building unchallenged. This type of structure had served us well in New Guinea and Biak, as well as on Luzon, but it had not been typhoon-tested. We learned later that the winds at the height of the storm had reached more than 150 m.p.h.

Although much of the roof was gone, including the sandbags the natives had teased us about, the rain was not coming in from the top. It was all horizontal and it was relentless. For two days and nights we huddled together, eating whatever canned food was available. At last, the wind slowed down to 70 m.p.h., and we decided to head for the 6th Group mess hall, a sturdier building. There we were served a good, hot meal.

We still had not received orders to move north to Korea. The news we did get was bad. Another typhoon was heading toward us and was thought to be as bad as the last one. We had just about dried out when the big winds came again, howling through our mesh and wire shelters. Once again we were soaked day and night.

On Okinawa, there were tombs with small openings dug into the hillsides, and we decided to escape the rains there. I crawled into one and inside I found three ornate ceramic pots, with matching covers. Their surfaces were covered with flower paintings and inside were the bones of the deceased. The custom was to lay the bodies in the tombs and then wait for seven years until the decaying process was complete. Then the bones were placed in the crocks for their final resting place.

The cave was about four feet high and quite deep. I set the pots outside to make room for Smoky and me. At least it was dry. During the night, the dog growled several times and I was sure I heard noises deep in the cave. It was unnerving. Cautiously, I lit a candle and saw eyes peering at us! Goats! One night of that was all I could take. In the morning, I returned the pots to the cave and went back to the mess hall. The storm was lessening and Hembury and I decided to get the hell out of there.

We gathered up Smoke and Duke, along with our soggy belongings, and, not telling the others, we hitch-hiked to the line. The moorings of the C-46 Cargo planes had loosened in the typhoon, so all their wing tips were battered and some rudders had blown off. Undamaged planes were flying in and we persuaded a pilot to take us back to Seoul with him. The Associated Press confirmed that five GIs had died during the first storm.

CHAPTER 8

SMOKY IN KOREA

We landed at Kimpo Airfield and called our squadron. We were sent a jeep to escort us to our new home. Japan had never been invaded. The island nation had been saved by the Big Winds on more than one occasion. In view of the strength of the storms that hit Okinawa, our invasion forces might have been in grave danger if the plan had gone forward.

The squadron in Korea was located in a farming area halfway between Inchon Harbor and Keijo, the Japanese name for Seoul. The officers were quartered in a schoolhouse a half-mile from the rest of us, who were housed in abandoned Japanese barracks. After nearly two years of tent living, this was a big improvement. It was October and we were near the 38th Parallel, no longer in the tropics, and we were COLD. The barracks, however, afforded us comfortable living space. There were four cots on each side of the room and two pot-bellied kerosene heating stoves in the center. At night, those sleeping closest to the stoves roasted. The muffled booms coming from inside the stoves wakened us often, and the little, black soot-balls belching from the stoves covered our blankets and everything else in the room. We did a lot of cleaning up.

The planes at Kimpo Airfield remained grounded. The typhoons hitting Okinawa had pushed the winds here up to 90 m.p.h. at 20,000 feet, even though we were hundreds of miles away. Our planes were ready to fly, though, with their cameras fully loaded. Everything had slowed to a stop now and we were just waiting...waiting for orders to go home. Every day we expected to hear something. About half the squadron remained sweating it out.

Truckloads of Japanese rifles, bayonets, pistols and swords were distributed to squadron members as souvenirs. As we were making preparations to leave Korea, I was going through my stuff. I emptied my barracks bags and found the cardboard letters I had used in trying to train Smoky to spell. This bag, made of heavy canvas which kept its contents dry, was sent by boat with the squadron to Korea. I thought I'd try them one more time. As I set the letters up on the entrance step to our room, the guys gathered around out of curiosity.

I mixed up the letters, M K 0 S Y, and commanded, "Smoky, spell your name." The little dog walked to the S and sat up. Coincidence, I thought. "Next," I ordered. She walked over and sat up in front of the M. "Good Lord," I muttered. "Next." She did the same with the 0. Then, on command, she sat up in front of the K and the Y! Everyone applauded. I grabbed her and hugged her and praised her for her wonderful feat. No one had ever seen anything like it.

She repeated her performance. It was amazing. I explained to my friends that I had tried to get her to do this when I was working with her on Luzon, but had abandoned the idea. The reason for her reluctance dawned on me now. I had been force training her and she hated it. Her revolt was her way of telling me, "When I'm ready, master. Only when I'm ready." Master? She had known all along what I was trying to teach her, but she had to remind me to keep my place. I understood that athletes needed some time away from practice to allow their enthusiasm for the game to return. Smoky's coach had learned his lesson. Smoky's attitude? "Nothing to it."

One of the guys. Earl Bartley, protested my control of the dog and said, critically, "Wynne, that poor dog can't defecate unless you say so! What the hell are you training her for?"

Surprised by his attitude, I replied, "I'm not sure. Maybe for show business when we get home."

He stared at me and then declared, "Your wife is gonna hate that dog!"

I hoped to take home some of the equipment we had put together for Smoky's tricks. But, my biggest concern was making sure that I could get the dog home. I had the vet's record of her shots, but I still thought I should conceal her when we boarded ship. Once again I would need some Yankee ingenuity.

I modified a oxygen mask carrying case. The green canvas bag came fitted with zippers and snaps. I cut a large hole in the bottom and tacked a screen over it. I had Smoky practice going in the zippered opening in the back of the bag and coming out the zippered opening in the front. I let her stay quietly in the bag for long stretches of time. It was soft and collapsible and adjusted easily to her movements. If she lay down, the bag lay down. If she stood up, the bag stood up. It was perfect.

One night, in the middle of the movie, the phone rang in the mess hall. The sound projector was turned off as Capt. Mac answered it.

"Yes, yes. Tomorrow? How many? Yes, sir!"

This was it, for sure. A cheer resounded in the small building. Capt. Mac announced that what we had heard was true. Over half of what was left of the squadron was being shipped out. He would read out their names and they would pack up and be ready to go in the morning.

The men were selected according a point system. We began to ready ourselves in case our names were called. Our new barracks bags were 1 1/4 times larger than our old ones, but we could only take one bag, so most of our equipment would have to stay behind.

My name was not on the list, but we got up early to watch the main contingent of the squadron load onto the trucks. They were wearing the new olive-drab-wool dress uniforms, the first we had been issued in two years. After the good-byes, two of us headed for the camera repair area in the basement of the Kimpo Airfield tower. Our 16 P-38s were gassed up and ready to take off, but no one was in the tower or anywhere else around the base.

A week passed with no change in my status. I decided to test my concealment plan. I put Smoky in her carrying case, along with some toilet articles and a pair of socks. I walked over to the mess hall and set the bag down. The cooks gathered around me and watched as I removed the socks and the bag of toiletries. Then I called out, "O.K.," and Smoky wriggled out of the case. We all had a good laugh and they agreed, "No one will know she's there."

No one had ever explained to me how to get a dog home. Army regulations stated, "No dog or mascot will go back to the U.S. on a War Department ship." At least that was what the scuttlebutt said. For two years I had been hearing about dogs taken off ships, or worse, being thrown overboard.

I was scared, I planned to keep her out of sight for the entire voyage. I figured if my buddies didn't know she was there, maybe the Skipper wouldn't catch on either. In our practice sessions. Smoky learned to sleep in the bag and grew fond of it because, when I put her in it, she knew we were going to go somewhere.

On November 1, the next call came and everyone, with the exception of some new arrivals, was on the list. We were going through the chow lines knowing that this meal would be the last one we would eat on foreign soil. The barracks were buzzing. We were scheduled to board ship at 7:00 a.m. and that night I wrote home, saying that this would probably be my last letter. We tried playing pinochle, but were too excited to concentrate and decided to hit the sack.

I crawled under my six blankets and Smoky snuggled close to me. I thought about seeing Margie again and wondered if I would be able to stay away from the phones when I landed. I wanted to surprise her. After two years away, I wanted to just walk in on her and give her a big hug.

At 3:30 a.m., CQ came around blowing his whistle and we bounced out of bed, shouting, "This is it! This is it!" We wolfed down pancakes, salty bacon and industrial strength coffee. But, everyone looked different—clean shaven and dressed in our new Olive Drabs with the snappy Eisenhower jackets.

After chow, the motor pool trucks pulled up and a mad rush of happy soldiers, yelling and laughing, scrambled into the vehicles. Hembury gave Duke to Shorty Randall because he did not have a home for the dog in the States. Hackman had his monkey in his ammo box.

At 6:00 a.m., we reached the area where the Air Corps men were assembled. We were all assigned to a commanding officer and loaded into trucks for the 25-mile ride to Inchon Harbor. Once again we were leaving towns and people we would never see again. Our emotions were a mixed bag of pity, regret and joy. I was still worried about Smoky.

All kinds of scenarios were spinning through my mind. Would she be discovered? What would happen then? I was carrying the letter Barbara Wood Smith had written about Smoky, along with photos showing the dog performing at hospitals. She was just a little pooch to those who didn't know her, but she meant a lot to those who did. Duke weighed about 25 pounds and Randall would have to carry him in plain view. I was sad for Hembury who had to give up his dog. As he watched Duke playing with Shorty in those last few days, I could see the regret showing plainly on his face.

The trucks rolled on to Inchon. All along the road, as far as we could see in all directions, were the GIs who had put in their two years in the tropics. These soldiers, their faces yellowed and their bodies worn out, managed to smile as we passed. I let Smoky out of her case for one more walk in this distant land. She was a comical sight in her navy turtleneck made from a wool, navy sweater sleeve. The cuff made the turtle neck, the back was left open and it had four holes cut to free her legs.

"Everybody over here!" someone shouted, and we grabbed our baggage and lined up for the march to the dock. As we loaded into the landing barges, I gave Ed Piwarski Smoky's bag to hold. It was lighter than our barracks bags and, because he had wrenched his back, I volunteered to carry the heavy stuff. The barges splashed out into Inchon Harbor, weaving through the other boats. I was still excited as we approached the big, dark-gray ship that was going to take us home. Passing around it to the other side, we could read its name, USS GENERAL WM. H. GORDON.

On the barge directly ahead of us, I could see a man struggling with something. It was Randall balancing Duke in his arms. An officer at the top of the gangway was shouting something at him. Randall continued up with Duke. The officer looked over a paper in his hand and waved him on. That barge moved away and ours took its place. I was hoping Smoky wouldn't move when Piwarski was walking past that officer. As he was passing him I was right behind and lugging our heavy bags on board. The gangplank was narrow and steep. I was about 10 steps from the top when the bags slipped and wedged around my knees, stopping me in my tracks. I was wrestling with my load and someone was yelling, "Hurry up! Hurry up!" I looked up and the officer was coming toward me. He lifted one of the bags and I continued up with the other. I explained to him that one of my buddies had strained his back and couldn't carry the heavy load. Smoky made it!

After climbing to the top deck, I followed the arrows down three decks to our sleeping quarters. The bunks were stacked five high and I grabbed a top bunk way back in a corner. Piwarski gave Smoky back to me and I set her on the bed, still in the bag. The loading process took all night and by morning, there were 5,000 men on board. There is very little space available on a crowded ship. There were only two meals a day and not many freshwater showers during our 10-day voyage.

That evening, before we sailed, the loudspeaker crackled and this announcement was made, "Will the man who brought the dog on board report to the troop office." My heart nearly stopped. I pitied poor Randall. Something surely must be wrong. The guys around me looked up and I crossed my fingers. A half-hour later, Randall came back, looking very worried. He told me the troop commander had ordered him to take his dog ashore. As he left the troop office, a sailor had come around the corner and asked him if he was the one who owned the dog. The sailor offered to hide Duke in the hold of the ship. He said he had hidden two other dogs there and thought he could fit in one more. The skipper of the ship didn't mind his crew having dogs aboard, but the Transport Commander was strictly Army and had more rigid views.

At high tide, the ship moved out of Inchon Harbor. The water got rougher and I got sicker. As long as the ship continued to roll, I would be helpless. Piwarski brought me a couple of oranges, and I managed to keep them down, but I was a no-show for meals. Some of the men from the 26th took Smoky up on deck for toilet trips and formed a ring around her to keep her out of sight. The sea got even rougher and I continued to miss chow calls. I saw no point to waiting in long lines, eating standing up and then losing my lunch before I could get back to bed. On the fourth day out, Smoky's presence was still generally a secret. It was late morning, and we had completed our chores and straightened our bunks, when the public address system bellowed, "All men on board who have brought either dogs or monkeys, report to the ship's office immediately!"

Once again, I froze. How could they know I had a dog on board? Maybe they were guessing. "Oh, well. I guess I'd better see what the boss has to say." Staggering out of the sack, reeling and feeling light headed, I made my way to the troop office. I was surprised to see five other men there.

The troop commander was yelling, "No dogs and especially no monkeys go back on this ship!"

A soldier was pleading with him, "But these are war dogs, sir, and I have a letter from Colonel..."

"I don't care if you have a letter from General MacArthur himself, you can't take any dogs back," the commander replied. I was feeling sicker by the minute.

The commander started up again. "Do you know what it will cost to bring a dog into the States," he shouted? "A thousand dollars—that's what the authorities will demand!"

"But, sir," the soldier protested, "I have a thousand dollars."

I was so ill by that time that I had to go back to my bunk. I determined then and there that I would not volunteer any information about Smoky. I would keep her out of sight. Every guy in the outfit offered to loan me whatever money they had so that I could buy her way into the States, if it came to that. Later, we found out that the troop commander was using scare tactics to get the men to dispose of their pets. We also learned that a bonding company would have put up the entrance fee and arrange a payment schedule the men could afford.

On the seventh day, the ship's officers were searching for two GIs who had been scheduled to leave the ship in Korea, but who had stowed away. A Navy lieutenant came down to our level and was walking through slowly when he spotted Smoky.

"Whose dog is that," he demanded. The men pointed sheepishly at me. He asked me if the dog was registered on the ship.

"No, sir," I answered.

"Did you hear them pipe it on the P.A. system?" he asked. "Yes, sir," I confessed, "but, I've been too seasick to report. I haven't made it to chow but twice since we started, sir." I must have looked bad enough to verify the story, because he believed me. I promised to go up when he called. An hour later, I was summoned to the ship's office. They told me I might have to pay the bond and asked if I was willing to do so.

I agreed, gladly, and they asked me to take an oath. I raised my right hand and swore that I was "telling the truth, the whole truth and nothing but the truth, so help me, God." The ship's captain and I both signed a paper that cleared the USS WM. H. GORDON of any responsibility for "One dog." A great weight was lifted from my shoulders. I showed the guys the paper and we all agreed that my worries were over. The monkeys they found were all put to sleep, but all the dogs were permitted to sail on.

I finally got my sea legs and began to eat regular meals. We spent the last days of our voyage on deck, although the sea was far from calm. We were taking the Great Circle route at a full 30 knots an hour. Our skipper was determined to break his own speed record from Korea to Washington State. This route took the ship high off Japan, past the Aleutian Islands and down the Canadian coast. The GORDON had been sent out for the invasion, but fortunately for all aboard it was almost home instead.

When the deck was uncrowded, I climbed onto a canvas-covered hatch and put Smoky through some other routines for the men who were standing around. Once I spotted the skipper and the troop commander watching from the bridge and smiling. The sailors brought Duke up every day and he and Smoky bounced around together.

On the 10th day, sea gulls swarmed around our fantail and Smoky barked furiously every time they came in close. At dawn on the 12th morning, we passed through the islands of Puget Sound. A small boat came toward us loaded with women and girls in bright-colored clothing. There was a little band with them and they were waving and singing. They were holding up signs that read, "WELL DONE! WELCOME HOME!" Our guys were going wild, hanging from the rigging and from the lifeboats. Not too many men showed up for chow that day.

When it was time to disembark, Piwarsky was able to carry his own bag. I put Smoky in her case and stowed my Japanese rifle and bayonet in the barracks bag. The line started moving forward, and slowly we snaked our way through the passageways and out on deck until, at last, we could see the gangplank. As we stepped off onto our Great Land, onto our own soil, we saw the customs inspector and the other brass lined up along the way, smiling in greeting as we passed by. A band was playing Sousa's "Stars and Stripes Forever." No one even tried to stop us for inspection. We were hustled into trucks for the pleasant ride through the streets of Tacoma and on to Fort Lewis.

We were sorted out according to separation centers and given our bed assignments in genuine U.S. Army barracks after two years of living in army tents. Then on to chow where FRESH MILK and T-BONE STEAKS were ours for the asking. Smoky had a bit of milk and a little piece of steak, and then she curled up on the bunk and fell asleep for the first time in her new homeland, AMERICA!

SMOKY — Parachutist Nadzab, New Guinea, 1944.
Photo/Howard Kalt

Back row L to R —
Bill Wynne and Edward
Downey who found Smoky.
Front row — Papuans.

L to R George Harsa, "Pal" and author 1938.
George was killed in a B-17 crash in 1943, Pal
disappeared shortly after.   Photo/Oscar Laisy

FIRST — Helmet Photo was used by YANK Magazine 1944. "Best Mascot, SWPA" Photo/Bill Wynne

JUNGLE TRIO — L to R AUTHOR, Smoky and Don Esmond, Nadzab, New Guinea, 1944. Photo/Howard Kalt

**FIFTH AIR FORCE VETERAN — Smoky
Yank Magazine's SWPA Champ Mascot
Photos/John Aikin**

BLANKET — Made out of a card table cover for Smoky in Brisbane, Australia by Red Cross Volunteers because after being in New Guinea so long she was cold. She wore it on combat missions for the same reason. Photos/John Aikin

COLONEL TURBO
Famous mascot
of the 25th Photo
Reconnaissance
Squadron.
Courtesy/Herman
Sunderman

PROUD SMOKY — I hold her surprise two day old pup "Topper." Smoky lost her Good Conduct Medal for a year. Photo/John Aikin

SMOKY AND TOPPER — Within three months Topper died as a disease wiped out about 30 other Sq. dogs in one week. Photo/John Aikin

F-5 "Anne II" flown by 26th Photo Co., Major Walter
Hardy — New Guinea 1944   Photo/Unknown

JAPANESE "DINAH" Photo Recon plane
captured at Hollandia.   Photo/Unknown

OA-10, USAAF version of PBY5A in which Smoky
flew 12 long combat missions from Biak Is. with
the 3rd Emergency Rescue Sq.
Photo/USAF Museum Dayton, Ohio

3RD Emergency Rescue Plane piloted by Capt. Victor Kregel with whom we flew several missions. Photo/ Victor Kregel Collection

JOLLY ROGERS — Strike Balikapapin Borneo oil fields as we circle for possible rescue in OA-10. Photo/USAF Museum Dayton, Ohio.

TYPICAL — 3rd ERS crewmen save an Australian P-40 pilot. Photo/Victor Kregel Collection

CREW — 3rd ERS holding Smoky after a Philippine mission. Photo/Bill Wynne

PALS — Jim Craig of the 41st Div. Combat Engineers holds Smoky. They met at the 3rd Field Hosp. in Nadzab. Craig rec'd the Legion of Merit at Hollandia. Photo/Frank Petrilac

SMOKY— This famous photo was taken in our tent on Biak Is., while sharing the coral rock with 5000 enemy hiding around the island and in caves.
Photo/John Aikin

"SALTY AS THE NAVY" said the crew of LST 706 in the South China Sea. Rust covered, her hair salt gummed, Smoky stands in a helmet in the South China Sea before 2 kamikazes were shot down by LST 706. The dalmatian belonged to the 391st Night Fighter Sq. Photo/John Aikin

NEAR MISS — A short fall 20mm shell coming from the right side passed two feet over our heads and hit four feet away into the lip of the round ventilator housing, Arrow "A." We were untouched as we ducked next to the jeep tire, Arrow "B," on the first of four kamikaze attacks. Eight men were wounded including 26th photo N.H. Smith facing camera at left. Photo/John Aikin

SCOOTER — Carved with a jungle knife from an orange crate and using P-38 control cable pulleys as wheels, Smoky performs on stage on Luzon. (Note the handmade tin footlight reflectors at the bottom foreground of the stage.) Photo/John Aikin

HYPO BARREL— Used for shipping photo chemicals, this drum was cut down for Smoky to walk on. Biak Is. 1944 Photo/Bill Wynne

PAINTED — The squadron painter decorated the drum on Luzon for Smoky to perform. Photo/Bill Wynne

HERO SMOKY — A dog of a thousand faces, poses for her story in WING DING, the 91st Photo Wing paper.

LINE PULLER — Smoky is set in position to pull a string through an eight inch diameter culvert going under a 60' wide taxi strip at Lingayen Gulf. Communications cables were then attached to the string and drawn through. Photos/John Aikin

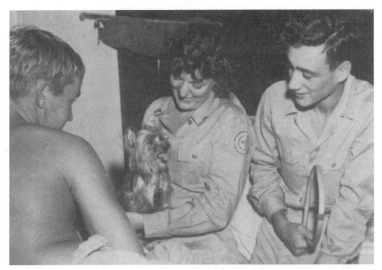

SMOKY — is held by American Red Cross nurse Barbara Wood Smith while visiting sick and wounded soldiers at the 120th General Hospital at Santo Tomas University campus in Manila in June 1945.
Photo/Dora Jane Hamblin ARC

CHICAGO 1946 — In clown suit made of a cargo chute by filipinos, Smoky visits war disabled at Gardener General Hospital. She also performed at Great Lakes Naval Hospital. Photo/American Red Cross

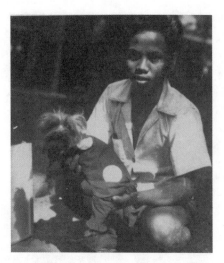

PHILIPPINES — A filipino boy holds the little dog in a clown suit made from a scrap cargo parachute by women needing new US made pesos. Photo/Bill Wynne

DEAD DOG — Smoky practices playing "dead" for Korean children near Kimpo Air Drome in October 1945.

"HOME FROM THE WARS" — Four photos and a Page One Story in the Cleveland PRESS appeared Dec. 7, 1945. She was an immediate national sensation.

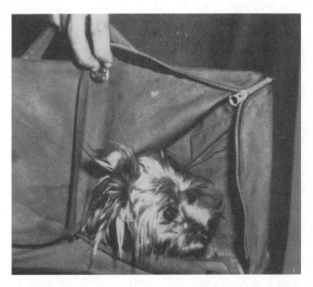

HIDDEN — Smoky was carried home hidden in a flight oxygen mask carrying case. For years after, many published stories in books, magazines, newspapers, newsreels and appearances in radio and television gave her more prominence than any dog of WWII.   Photos/Nash-Knipper, Cleveland Press

THE REAL JOB — During 1947-53 in show business among other work, the author flew Flight Icing Research missions with the National Advisory Committee for Aeronautics (NACA) later NASA. The WWII B-24 Liberator (note jet engine under wing) and B-25 Mitchell bombers were the most de-icible planes in the world. The equipment tested on these extremely hazardous flights is still in use on all commercial and military planes 50 years later. It is said no plane has ever been lost using these anti-icing and de-icing devices. Photos/NACA/NASA Lewis

CONVENTION — We perform at the National Convention of the America Humane Societies. 1950 Photo/American Humane Assoc.

TIGHT WIRE — On apparatus made from scrap airplane parts, an oil drum and steel tubing, our tightwire walker finds her way while blind-folded at Luzon, 1945.

PARMADALE ORPHANAGE — A resident from 1928-30, the author returns with Smoky to perform for the children of the village. The wire act was always the grand finale of performance.
Photo/Glenn Zahn, Cleveland Press

MATINEE IDOLS — Patch, Bill Wynne and Smoky, the trio that played many Saturday matinees and New Year Eves for years throughout Ohio.
Photo/Charles Williams

OUT OF RETIREMENT — Smoky stars in "How To Train Your Dog" at 9:00 a.m., Sunday mornings on WNBC Channel 3 in Cleveland, 1954. Photo/Art Laufman

PIONEER — Smoky appears in very early T.V. We appeared on all three Cleveland Channels 3, 5, 9; 1948-1954. We appeared weekly in a children's show on CH. 9, now Ch. 8, titled "Castles in the Air" for 42 weeks live and never repeated a trick. Photo/Albert Jecko

OUR FAMILY THEN — Back row L to R Bobby 3, Marcia 4, Billie 6. Front row L to R Joanne 7, holding Smoky age 12, Donna 2, Susan 5, and Caesar mini poodle 6.   Photo/Bill Wynne

IS THIS SMOKY? — Lt. Grace G. Heidenreich, U.S. Army nurse holds "Christmas" shortly before her yorkie pup was lost in Dobodura, New Guinea in 1944.
Photo/Grace Heidenreich Collection

PLAYBILL — A typical newspaper ad strip of theatrical attractions
of the late '40s and early '50s.   Cleveland Plain Dealer

CONFLICT — "The other woman was a REAL dog!" Margie and Smoky at the Western Reserve Classic Dog Show 1946. We had been engaged since 1943 and then the four lb. dog came along in the middle of the war. Margie says the fame affected the rest of our lives. Here Smoky has just won all the ribbons for her then rare breed as she was the first Yorkshire Terrier entered in the WRKC show in nine years. We also performed at center ring before the Best in Show judging. Photo/Ray Matjasic, PLAIN DEALER

PART TWO

"One consolation of being
poor is you have to dream
all of this up."

Anne of Green Gables (film)

CHAPTER 9

A NEW LIFE

The next morning, we were greeted by the rest of the 26th who had just arrived on the USS Marine Flasher, a slower ship than the Gordon, which had left Korea a week before us. It was a great reunion. We never expected to meet again in the Army. At chow that morning, I noticed the KPs were all prisoners of war. The Germans looked so healthy and muscular compared to our guys who were gaunt and yellowed from atrabine. At first glance, one might have thought that we had lost the war and these Germans had won.

After several days of processing, we were ready to board the troop trains. Those of us going to Camp Atterbury near Indianapolis (the separation center closest to Ohio) boarded a train with many soldiers from Infantry, Signal Corps, Tank Corps, etc. The train had sleeper cars and kitchen cars. Four days on a train was a new experience for our mascot. It would stop often enough to pick up water for the steam engine for relief for Smoky. There was fresh meat at meals, and the sleeper bed converted from the car seat beat sleeping on a canvas cot anytime.

Some of us would pull KP duty on the four-day cross-country trip, but we didn't mind—our time in the Army was just about over. Poor Randall, after all he had gone through to bring Duke home, he lost the dog somewhere in Fort Lewis.

At Camp Atterbury, we were assigned barracks and told that in two days we would be discharged. I called my mother for the second time. I had telephoned her from Tacoma, but asked her not to tell Margie about the call.

After our physicals and dental examinations, we were approached by an officer who wanted to recruit us for the Reserves. We had been overseas for two years, and we almost booed the guy out of the hall. "All right, all right," he complained and left without giving us his pitch.

On November 27, 1945, our discharge papers were issued and we were released with civilian-train money and mustering-out pay, which included 30 days' pay for each year's furlough time we had not received. As members of the 26th Photo, we were also issued the Asiatic Pacific Campaign ribbon and eight Battle Stars, Philippine Liberation ribbon with a Battle Star, the Victory Medal with Battle Star and Good Conduct Medal. There was a Presidential Unit Citation Ribbon with Oak Leaf Cluster on the right side of our blouses and four horizontal gold bars representing two years of overseas duty. In addition. Smoky and I wore silver crewmen wings.

Don Esmond and John Vellos, also from Cleveland, suggested that we postpone our departure for a day and go to a barber shop in Indianapolis for a haircut and joked about the pampering, but decided to go for it. The next day, as we sat waiting for the Cleveland train, some of the Indianapolis USO troupe spotted Smoky and walked over to pet her. I told them her story and one of them called the Indianapolis Star. A wire service picked up the story and ran it with the photo (taken on Luzon) of Smoky in her clown suit, riding her scooter.

Later, as our train neared the Union Terminal in downtown Cleveland, it stopped to pick up an electric engine at the west side Linndale yards. Linndale was near my home and, as I sat there, eager for the train to move on, I heard someone call out, "Is Bill Wynne here?"

It was my cousin, Sonny Adler, although I almost didn't recognize him. "Gosh, Sonny, have you grown!" I laughed. I had last seen him when he was 13, and now he was a strapping sixteen-year-old! He was all grown up and told me he preferred to be called Chuck. He said my mother was waiting out in the car and they would drive me home. After saying good-bye to my buddies, I hurried off the train.

What a joyful reunion that was! I had not seen my mom since 1943. In July of that year, I had been given a furlough because Mom was scheduled for emergency surgery. I had given Margie her engagement ring at the same time. Later, in October, Mother and Margie had come to visit me at Seymour Johnson Field in Goldsboro, North Carolina, just before I shipped out.

Now, at last, I was going home. I couldn't wait to surprise Margie, who lived just ten houses from my home. I knocked on the door and then let Smoky wander into the living room. Margie cried, "Oh, nooo!" as the little dog paraded up to her. Is there a word in any language to appropriately describe the reunion of loved ones at the return from war?

Back at my house I wondered if my big shepherd, Toby, would remember me. In one of Albert Payson Terhune's dog books, the author had asked if a dog could recognize someone after two years. I would soon find out. At first, Toby seemed puzzled, but when I sat down, he came to my side. I talked to him and he wagged his tail half-heartedly and whined. I talked to him some more.

My brother, Jim, called out, "Bill! Bill!" and Toby began to jump all over me. It was great! Over the years, Jim had been saying my name out loud and Toby always responded by looking around for me. Now I was really there, and my dog and I were happy to be together again.

Smoky had another new companion at home. Lucky was a big, bright, black cat and very special to me. Before I left for the service, Lucky had taken long walks with Margie and me at night. His favorite snoozing spot was on the front window sill. To get there he'd leap five and one half feet to the top of the upright piano, jump down behind it to the radiator and stroll across the lamp table to his perch. He was also a thief and could open the icebox just by lifting the handle. After I put hooks and eyes on each of the wooden doors, he learned to lift those as well. Rubber bands stretched between the latches and hooks proved to be no problem for him. He just plucked at them with his claws until they broke. Now, Mom had a refrigerator and Lucky was out of luck.

After I had been home for a week, Mom told me that Maxwell Riddle, the dog columnist for the Cleveland Press, had phoned and wanted me to get in touch with him as soon as possible. Max was in the hospital at the time, but another reporter was eager to interview us and asked me to bring in my dog the next day.

I carried Smoky into the Press city room in her bag. I was in uniform, wearing my ruptured duck (discharge button) on my blouse. Smoky's button was on her blanket. The reporter introduced herself as Eleanor Prech as she led the way to her desk. After sitting down, I zipped open the bag and the little dog squeezed out and walked straight to Eleanor, who was taken aback by Smoky's sudden appearance.

She asked me how I got Smoky, who found her, where she was found and where we had been together. Within minutes, the other reporters had gathered around the desk and Eleanor asked me to have Smoky show them some of her tricks. It was exciting, but all the attention made me nervous. The city editor, Lewis Clifford, was as impressed as the others. He called for a photographer and whispered to him, "Get all you can on this. It's a great story."

We went into the photo studio and photographers Glenn Zahn and Bud Nash took some shots of Smoky, first in her coat-blanket and then in the carrying case. They tied two pieces of string to some chairs and Smoky walked the tight rope for them. I formed a hoop with my arms and she jumped through it. They took five photos in all.

The next day, December 7, 1945, we all looked at the Press in disbelief. There on Page One, the headline, TINY DOG HOME FROM THE WAR, had pushed aside the news of General Yamashita's death sentence. There were four pictures and the story on the front page in the home edition. The full account was big news in all editions that day and our phone began ringing off the hook.

One of the first calls was from Captain Arthur Roth of the Police Department. Captain Roth had worked with juveniles for many years. Back when I was in grade school, he had come around with the famous German Shepherd, Silver King, an honorary police dog in 25 cities. The dog wore badges from all 25 on his harness as he traveled around the country giving demonstrations about traffic safety. Captain Roth asked if I would do some Christmas shows with him in a neighborhood with a high delinquency rate. I was honored. For a week, uniformed officers in a police cruiser picked us up daily. We were chauffeured to the theater where Captain Roth entertained the kids. There I met the Cleveland Safety Director, Anthony Celebreeze, who proudly displayed his ruptured duck on his lapel. Celebreeze later became one of Cleveland's most popular mayors and eventually served on the Ohio Supreme Court.

Many local companies and fraternal organizations were planning Christmas shows. We were taking calls daily from program chairmen of these organizations. I booked them all. I wasn't sure what to charge for a performance, so I asked for $10 to $25. (We performed with or without payment.) After the Press story hit the wire services, we appeared in newspapers in most major U.S. cities. The Scranton paper ran four photos in its Sunday magazine.

A popular radio broadcaster, Bob Neal, had a program called "Sport Spotlight of the Week." Bob had asked me to be his guest. I thought he was kidding. It was our first live radio show. Henry Leffingwell, the host of a Saturday radio show about dogs, interviewed us next. Leffingwell was the head of the Animal Protective League of Cuyahoga County and I worked with him many times after that.

We were getting lots of experience, but our equipment was limited. I was able to get a drum for Smoky to walk on. I glued a long sheet of sandpaper to the drum to give her better traction. A sign painter put the 5th Air Force symbol on one side and the 26th Photo insignia on the other. During our Christmas shows we were introduced as "Bill Wynne and his dog, Corporal Smoky." I came onstage carrying the case, and began,

"When I headed home from overseas, someone asked, 'What's in the bag?' I replied, 'Just some toilet articles.' But, when my buddies inquired, 'Where is it?' I said, 'It's in the bag.'"

At that point, I pulled open the bag's zipper and out trotted Smoky, drawing a surprised gasp from the audience. Then I told them how my buddy had found her in a foxhole in New Guinea and how I bought her for two pounds Australian or $6.44 American. I described the 12 combat missions she flew with me from Biak to Borneo to the Philippines. I bragged about her pulling the string under the airstrip on Luzon and how she surprised us with a two-ounce pup on Biak. I boasted of her status as First Prize Mascot of Yank Magazine in the SWPA in 1943 and told them of her training program in the New Guinea jungle, the Biak Island coral reef and in Luzon, Okinawa and Korea. To close the act, I knelt down with the case and Smoky rushed back into it and I lifted her high in the air. We were a big success.

Sometimes we had band accompaniment. The numbers I had selected for Shacklette to play overseas were the ones we still used in the act. "Pretty Baby" as the dog walked through my legs. "Funeral March" as she played dead, and so on. In show business, the tradition was to use animal acts as openers. If we were on a bill for more than one performance, the directors who took note of the audience response, inevitably switched us to the closing act. They loved us.

We worked with both amateurs and professionals. It was an exciting time. I discovered that Smoky was a big ham. She realized that she could get away with things on stage that I would not tolerate when we practiced alone. Sometimes when she was jumping her three hurdles, she ran around the middle one or skipped the third one entirely. The audience loved it and responded with bursts of applause, so I pretended not to see it. We worked those short cuts into the act and always drew appreciative laughter. If the booking agent knew us, he always booked us as the closing act. People came to us after our shows and told me about their dogs. Children asked for autographs and the newspapers continued to run photos and stories.

Crile Hospital was a local Army hospital filled with soldiers from every theater of operations, recovering from wounds and disabilities. We performed there on several occasions. First, we performed on stage in the

81

day room for those who were ambulatory and then in some of the wards for those who were not.

One day, the nurses wheeled several men into the day room and placed them up front. We began to perform and, suddenly, one of the patients in a wheelchair began gurgling and bouncing about in his chair. He held out his arms, and one of the nurses asked me to give him the dog. He held Smoky in his arms and began smiling and swinging her back and forth. The nurses were crying. They told me later that the soldier had been catatonic and hadn't responded to any stimulus, in fact, had not even moved for two years. That was the first positive sign he had shown, and they were overcome with emotion.

In February 1946, I contacted the Al Sirat Grotto Circus. The circus performed yearly at the Public Hall in Cleveland. Most of the acts had already been booked for that year's show, mostly from the Barnum and Bailey Circus. The guy in charge had seen our publicity and decided to try us as a concert, an act that performed after the regular circus concluded. I signed a contract to perform during an eight-day run. My fee was to be $200.

I was eager to set up the tightwire apparatus before our circus performance. My high-school friend, Jack Lewis was sure that his friends, the Lovejoys could help me. So many times I received willing help from others when I could not manage something on my own, and to all those good people I will always be grateful.

Margie and I had met the Lovejoys' son, George (Babe), on a triple date in 1942, just before he was shipped overseas with the 37th Division. Babe was sure that he wasn't going to come back home. He died on Luzon. Their other son, John, was in and out of Army hospitals for years, suffering from war-related stress.

Mr. Lovejoy was a carpenter and thought he could build a tightwire rig by my deadline. We worked together on the design so that it could be transported by car and assembled at the performance site. The rig was painted red and white and looked really first class. He even made a little ladder for Smoky.

He refused any money. Jack suggested that I try to find Mr. Lovejoy a Meerschaum corn cob pipe because his were burned out. Because of the war, new ones were not available. I sent a request to the Meerschaum factory, along with a brief explanation of our situation, and they sent me, free of charge, 24 brand-new corn cob pipes and stems. Mr. Lovejoy was thrilled.

At the Public Hall, our dressing room was upstairs and away from the auditorium. The faces of many opera, stage and movie stars had been reflected while making up by the light bulbs surrounding the mirror. Here we were. Smoky on the powder table getting her hair brushed. We had to run back and forth to keep track of the show. When standing near the main wing, I held on tight to Smoky, trying to keep her as calm as possible. She could smell the wild animals and could hear the roaring of the lions and tigers as we passed the cages along the halls encircling the arena. Also, I knew that elephants are not fond of dogs, and this circus had 50 elephants!

In the middle of the show, the clowns, including Emmett Kelly himself, burst out onto the stage. They began firing cannons and Smoky started spinning at the sound, the way she had done during air alerts and ack-ack firing overseas. She became very nervous and I took her outside the building until the cannons were finished. There are fewer places any colder than Cleveland's lakefront at 20 degrees with high humidity. The wet cold penetrates everything you are wearing. We had to stay outside during every performance until the clown act was over.

The last concert act that the circus had tried was a rodeo and it proved to be a disaster. The agent hoped our show would hold people's interest and so our act was promoted during the regular three-ring circus. The opening show ran much too long, nearly four hours. There were many little children in attendance and after four hours they were sleepy and wanted to go home. When our turn came to go on, there were 17 people left in the 5,000-seat auditorium.

As the band played "From the Halls of Montezuma," a Marine in full dress marched out. With "Anchors Aweigh," a sailor appeared. A soldier paraded out to the center ring to the tune of "The Caissons Are Rolling Along." Our turn came next to the strains of the "Army Air Corps Song." We did our little show with the band playing our tunes. Our small audience applauded enthusiastically, but the clapping was barely audible in the huge auditorium.

The following performances were equally disappointing. By the fourth day, I heard that our show was folding. It did. I went to get my $200 and found 10 Masonic representatives sitting around a table. (Al Sirat is a Masonic order.) I was told that I would receive a compromise amount of $100. "Wait a minute," I said, "I signed a contract for $200." The man who headed the Grotto Circus replied, "Yes, but we never signed the contract." As I examined my copy, I realized that he was right. No one from the circus had signed it.

The whole affair disgusted me. They had made a postcard with Smoky's footprint on it and planned to sell it to the audience. Someone phoned my mom and told her the organization did not plan to pay me a percentage from the sales. When I inquired about this, the head man told me angrily that they wouldn't display the postcards at all. He was furious that some anonymous tipster had warned me about it.

Later, another circus owner asked me to sign with his outfit. "No thanks! Definitely not interested!" was my response. I never told my friends at the Cleveland Press about this fiasco. I still hoped that some of the other Masonic lodges might sign us up for local performances. My instincts were correct. We played for hundreds of Masonic groups and every experience was a pleasant one. Those later contacts made up for the great discouragement I felt after the circus.

Max Riddle was program chairman of the Cleveland Classic, the Western Reserve Kennel Club's two-day benched show. Max asked us to perform just before the Best in Show competition. I had never been to a big dog show before, but I was surprised that we would be considered an attraction. Although we were rushed because the show was running long, things went well. We attracted the attention of C.E. Harbison of the Kennel Rations company and Harry Miller of the Gaines dog foods. Miller later proposed to his parent company, General Mills, that they hire us to give demonstrations at schools in New York State, but he couldn't convince them. I always wished we could have worked something out. I know it would have been a good thing for all concerned.

We were still receiving many letters from other dog owners. One world traveler wrote to say that he never went anywhere without his Yorkie. Another letter came from Goldie Stone, a well-known Yorkie breeder from Columbus, Ohio. She had read about us, too. Goldie wrote that, from the newspaper photos, she could see that Smoky was a very typy dog. This meant that she was a very good specimen of the breed. We also heard from two other Yorkie owners in our own area.

Goldie's life story was fascinating. She and her husband, Charlie, had been featured circus performers. Goldie's father was the founder of the Fothergill Amusement Company. When Charlie and Goldie married in 1910, they billed themselves as Stone and Stone and played circuses, fairs and amusement parks. Later they toured in Vaudeville. Their specialties were tightwire walking and a balancing act. They were very successful and played year-round, a rare accomplishment in those days. An unfortunate fall by Charlie cut their careers short.

On the bill with them at one time was a 200-pound woman with a five-pound Yorkie named Mike. They were billed as a song and dance act. Goldie learned to love Mike and decided to breed Yorkies when they left show business. Their Petite Yorkshire Terrier Kennel was founded in 1929. Eventually, they owned 18 champions, which Goldie herself handled at dog shows. Her Champion Petite Magnificent Prince was the first American-bred and home-bred Yorkshire to win Best in Show.

Goldie invited us to come to visit her in Columbus. Margie, Smoky (in her case) and I traveled there by train. The Stones lived in a simple, circa 1910 bungalow. The decor was from the late 1920s and much of Goldie's lace handwork trimmed the furniture. When I set Smoky down, Goldie whistled and said, "Mr. Wynne, I don't believe you realize what a fine dog you have there. If that dog were in my kennel and 10 weeks old, I could get $250 for her!" She speculated about Smoky's ancestry, mentioning Harringay and Haslington stock. As usual, the question of how she got to New Guinea came up.

Goldie's dogs had unbelievably long hair, some of it braided and some of it tied up in Chinese tissue, with mustaches, sideburns and all. Goldie demonstrated how to wrap the hair up in four small bunches on each side of the dog after combing out the hair. A wet comb keeps the hair ends from splitting, Goldie said. When let down, her champion dog's hair was seven inches longer than the dog's height, and trailed behind like a bridal train. Of her 16 Yorkies, five had the run of the house. In their basement, cages were table-high and pens on the floor were covered with newspaper. A medicine cabinet, refrigerator and some grooming tables completed the workplace. There was no dog odor whatsoever in the house. Outside, there were two fences around the yard, one about two feet inside the other. This kept neighborhood dogs from touching noses with her Yorkies. I would not necessarily recommend Goldie's method of protecting her dogs from communicable disease, but it certainly worked for her. Her dogs never had any shots. At shows, the dogs' noses and footpads were wiped with alcohol as soon as they were lifted from the floor after the walking and running demonstrations. She carried her own table to show them on.

Smoky was the only outside dog the Stones had ever permitted to enter their house without a quarantine. (Of course, Smoky never went near any of the other dogs.) If a dog was brought in for breeding, it was kept isolated at first. Goldie never lost a dog because of communicable illness. Surprisingly, the Stones never owned a car and relied on the kindness of friends to get them to the dog shows.

Very tiny Yorkies, usually the result of breeding small parents, were sold at top prices. Goldie told me that this can be risky to the mother. Brood bitches are generally larger, about seven pounds. The males weigh under four pounds. The parents produce both large and small dogs with different qualities of show conformation. The more imperfect offspring are sold as pet stock or as brood matrons. However, even pet stock can throw some fine specimens.

A friend brought over her Yorkie, a one-pound adult standing four inches high. It was unbelievable. Yorkies weighing one pound are fragile and require special care. "The Guinness Book of Almost Everything You Didn't Need to Know About Dogs," which also lists Smoky (Smokie), says that the smallest dog on record was a Yorkie that weighed four ounces. It lists another Yorkie that stood two-and-one-half inches tall. To such tiny ones, a fall down the stairs or a human misstep could prove fatal. We remained friends with the Stones and, over the years, Goldie often encouraged me to write this story.

Early in 1946, Smoky was scheduled to meet Sinbad, the mascot of the U.S. Coast Guard. (A newspaper strike prevented any publicity about the meeting.) A chief petty officer had written a book about the adventures of Sinbad, who resembled a Rottweiler. My friend, Jack Lewis, a fellow photographer from our high school days, was the official Coast Guard photographer in Cleveland. Jack had served in the Far Pacific and had survived a number of kamikaze attacks off Okinawa. He was daffy about Smoky and almost succeeded in ruining her discipline by trying to get her to do tricks for him. Because he was a pal and so good to us over the years, I overlooked this interference.

During the promotion for the Sinbad book. Jack asked me to bring Smoky down to the Coast Guard Lighthouse Station on Cleveland's lakefront. Sinbad was there and Jack took some pictures. One was published in the Sunday Sun, a new paper that lasted only two weeks. Jack also set up a meeting with Catherine Cornell, who was in town playing Antigone. In "The Barretts of Wimpole Street," a Yorkie had played the part of Flush, Elizabeth Barrett's pet. Miss Cornell had traveled through Europe on a military tour with this play. The Barrett dog had been a Cocker Spaniel and, ordinarily, that was the breed used in the play. However, there was no Cocker Spaniel available for the tour, and a Yorkie owned by one of the girls in the company had learned the part in only one rehearsal. Miss Cornell was impressed by Smoky's temperament and was happy to pose with us for one of Jack's pictures.

I began work on my book at that time. I wrote in longhand and Mom and Margie edited and typed the manuscript for me. We worked this way for several months, hoping we might find a publisher. It was a blessing to record all the war-time experiences right then, because many of those memories dimmed over time.

A friend of the Stones, Rebecca Lawrence Lowrie, lived in Galesburg, Illinois, and owned two of Goldie's Yorkies. She was a reader for the Book of the Month Club and had a connection with Life Magazine. She hoped to generate interest in my book.

My uncle, John (Jack) M. Caffrey, was the manager of a small office of the John Hancock Insurance Company in Roseland, a suburb of Chicago. (He later built that office into the company's largest, employing 59 agents.) Uncle Jack wanted me to come to Chicago so that a meeting with the Lowries and other plans he had made could be coordinated. In Chicago, my uncle called the Daily News and Smoky and I were invited to come to the newspaper. They ran two nice photos with the story and mentioned the hospitals that we were planning to tour in the area. When we arrived at the Great Lakes Naval Training Base hospital, four news photographers were waiting for us. Someone asked, "How did you know they were coming?"

They answered in unison, "We read it in the Daily News!"

The Chicago Tribune, Chicago Sun and Herald American all ran stories about us. The Herald American assigned their special features writer, Elmar Brown, to cover the story. His lead paragraph read, "Smoky looks like the business end of your wife's favorite mop dyed in tobacco juice." We also performed at the Gardiner General Army Hospital.

In Cleveland, the newspaper editors would not touch a story if another local paper had printed it first. The Cleveland News and the Cleveland Plain Dealer stayed away from our story because the Press had given it the big Page One play. The three papers had very different readerships, but always pursued this policy nonetheless.

For the Chicago hospital tours, the Red Cross picked us up every day in a station wagon. We used the tightwire now. It had been shipped to us in a rough box made for us by the F. H. Hill Casket Co. in Cleveland.

We gave a private show for one young GI dying of cancer. We were asked to give a private show for some who were insane and locked behind bars. I was very nervous when one of these men asked to hold Smoky. I set her down, not knowing what she would do. She crawled between the bars when he called, wagging her tail and wriggling her back end, like she always did. He picked her up and, laughing, hoisted her into the air. As she passed his face, she swept his cheek with her friendly tongue. They were delighted with each other and she behaved as if they had been friends all their lives. He set her down and she slipped back to me between the bars. (I sighed in relief.) Others wanted to hold her, too, and, when it was time to leave, the last man set her down and all of them applauded, bringing a lump to my throat.

Phone calls came flooding in to Uncle Jack's house. One was from Frank Perko of the 26th, saying he had enjoyed the newspaper story. Uncle Jack called Freeman Wood, an insurance executive who was also on the Board of Trustees of the Chicago animal shelter, headed by the veterinarian, Dr. Young. One news photographer took a picture of Smoky with a homeless dog. These shelters need all the publicity they can get to help find homes for the animals. This photo was picked up by the wire services and used in newspapers throughout the country. Dr. Young shot promotional movies of us, and these films were used by the shelter for many years.

Mrs. Lowrie sent me the train fare from Chicago to Galesburg. When we arrived, a black limousine was waiting and a distinguished-looking man in a gray suit flagged us over. He introduced himself as James Carroll, business manager for the Lowries. Jim told me that he had been chief warden of Bilibid Prison in Manila until the war broke out.

The Lowrie mansion was on a slight hill and had been built in the 1880s. Mrs. Lowrie was a trustee of Smith College and Mr. Lowrie had gained prominence as a New York attorney. The household was maintained by four servants and the oldest of the staff was in her 80s. This lovely lady had been with the household since Mrs. Lowrie's birth. I was introduced to each one, and all were treated as family members. At dinner, the array of silverware confused me and Mrs. Lowrie's nanny saw my reluctance to begin using the flatware. She leaned over and whispered to me, "Just start with the left fork and work in."

We were entertained very graciously and felt welcome there. Smoky posed for pictures near a large globe to illustrate our world travels. Mrs. Lowrie explained that this homestead had been the family's base of operations for 37 tenant farms. A century-old map covering the wall illustrated the farms' locations in reference to the main house.

We discussed how Mrs. Lowrie would first contact A.B.C. Whipple, an associate editor of Life Magazine. That night I slept in a bed so deep I almost disappeared. They had suggested that Smoky stay with me the way the Lowrie dogs shared their masters' bedroom. It was hard for me to believe that a simple kid and his dog, just back from the tents and Army cots in the Pacific, could be enjoying such luxury.

The word from Mr. Whipple was that because they had already done three stories on war mascots, the Life editors did not feel another one was warranted. I was grateful for all that the Lowries had done, but, at that point, I gave up trying to get my book published. As I saw it then, people were tired of World War II. They had lived it. Those at home had suffered through rationing, the loss of loved ones and the damaged lives that long wars can generate. It was time to forget and get on with the postwar promises of a better world.

The Press sent me to see Julius Kemeny, the director of recreation for the City of Cleveland. He had two things going then that he thought might interest me. One was the Show Wagon, a traveling vaudeville show. The stage was mounted on a large truck that drove around to city playgrounds and parks on summer evenings. The other choice was to be master of ceremonies of the Traveling Zoo, a contingent of zoo animals scheduled to visit playgrounds all summer. The latter opportunity appealed to me more. It was a chance to perform four times a day, five days a week, tightening up our act, adding new training and getting paid for it. We made $40 a week. Kemeny took a special interest in us and his office was always open. I learned much later that he had lost his only son in the European campaign.

1946 was the Sesquicentennial Year in Cleveland and many special events were planned. As stars of the Zoo Wagon, Smoky and I were invited to sit on the dignitaries' platform during the Memorial Day celebration. We were seated between Louis B. Seltzer, editor of The Cleveland Press, and Charles Otis, who was in his 80s and had been named Mr. Cleveland for the celebratory year. Charlie, a fascinating man who had once owned the Cleveland News, told me a story about a Yorkshire Terrier he had owned. At the turn of the century, Yorkshires were very popular and Charlie's had caught the eye of Queen Victoria. The Queen wanted to buy the Yorkie, but Charlie steadfastly refused to part with his prize pet.

The Traveling Zoo's wagon was a trailer painted with colorful circus decorations. It was towed by a medium-sized flatbed truck, which carried stanchions and ropes for crowd control. The doors were horizontal and ran the length of the wagon. When open, the upper door was propped up like an awning and the lower door was dropped to show off animal cages. During my lectures, I was able to remove the animals from their cages for demonstrations. There was a small pen behind the cab for the pony that traveled with us.

Our little zoo had three sponsors: The Cleveland Zoo, which supplied the animals and attended to their care; The Cleveland Press, which covered events and provided our publicity; and the Cleveland Recreation Department, which set up schedules and paid my salary. We rode a bike for the three miles between our house and the zoo. Like most people after the war, we had no car. Manufacturers had barely begun civilian car production and every dealer had a long waiting list. Smoky rode in the front wire basket.

One of the denizens of our animal world was George, a rhesus monkey brought home from the Philippines, and he was a genuine nuisance. He unscrewed the wing nuts from the side panels of the wagon. At first, he stuffed them in his mouth, puffing out his cheeks. Getting them back was a real pain. We tried holding him upside down and shaking him. No dice. We made several trips with the sides banging in the open position and decided we had had enough. Two of us held him and forced his mouth open to retrieve the fasteners. After that, we kept the hardware out of sight in the pocket of Tom Byrne, our driver.

We had 16 animals, including a raccoon, a civet, an armadillo, a goat and the pony. The P.A. system blared "Some Day My Prince Will Come" and other numbers from Walt Disney's hit movie, "Snow White." Kids came from everywhere. The press recorded our every move. Many of the children had never seen live animals except for dogs and cats. With no money to spare, these kids could not afford the streetcar fare to visit the big Cleveland Zoo. Sometimes we drew more than a thousand people. We always met our four-shows-a-day schedule and never a had a sick animal. Byrne, a native Irishman, took on the tending of the animals.

The Downtown Rotary Club asked me to give a show to raise money for the Zoo, which always faced financial problems. I was told by the Zoo director, Fletcher Reynolds, to give our usual performance. Afterwards, I was criticized for not asking for money outright. The money came through, though, and Joe Cherry, the chief keeper told the others, "The kid did all right." The kid was doing all right and having a lot of fun in the bargain.

This show was performed at the Statler Hotel and had been seen by a local physician who came to me and asked me to select a dog for his children. He didn't specify a breed and said that even a mixed-breed pup would be fine. I preferred to dodge this request, not wanting to take on the responsibility. The doctor assured me repeatedly that if things did not work out, he would not blame me, so I finally agreed to try.

I called Henry Leffingwell at the APL and asked if I could come down someday before the shelter was open to the public. I wanted time to look at the dogs. I am always amazed at the fine quality of some of the dogs at the shelters. That day I was impressed by an alert, mostly Wire-haired Terrier. He was aggressive but not mean, friendly but not uncontrollable. I was in the process of making my decision about this dog when the doors opened and the first visitors of the day arrived. The dog was out of its cage and two boys, about six and eight years old, came over to pet him. The dog responded happily to their attention.

I paid the fee and took him to my veterinarians, Drs. Roberts and Wagner, who were among the very first to have a small animal practice. Dr. Wagner had been a cavalry veterinarian in France during World War I. In the mid-40s, Dr. Wallace Wendt joined their practice. They were reluctant to let me bring a dog from the APL into their hospital. I explained the situation and they agreed to hold him in quarantine for five days. He checked out fine.

We arranged to meet the physician and his two boys at the vet hospital. When the dog was let out of his cage, he ran to the boys and greeted them as if he had been theirs all along. It was a wonderful sight. I worried about the adoption for a week before the doctor called and told me what a great little dog it was. After that, the boys called me now and then to thank me and to say how happy they were with their pet. Some things work out right.

Mutual Radio Broadcasting called to inform me two former GIs were assigned to travel around the country in a jeep gathering interviews on the sites of business locations of former service people.

We were selected for interview along with Bob Feller, Ted Williams of baseball fame and a former WAC who started a cement mixing business. They were sticklers for script reading and I was strictly comfortable only with ad lib. We compromised with a combination of both, and the interviews aired.

Meanwhile, the Zoo Wagon was drawing record crowds. Smoky, of course, was the real star. We worked in some fancy Hollywood-style tricks. Sometimes we called up a volunteer from the audience and Smoky was ordered to stay with that person no matter where he or she went. Following my voice and my hand signals, she was able to work with strangers. On command, she jumped on their backs and sat up and "said prayers" against their thighs when they knelt down. This was good discipline for a show-biz dog and would serve us well later on, when we eventually headed for California.

We also did shows in the suburbs of Cleveland. Among the places we played was Parmadale, the orphanage where I had stayed as a child. I was happy to be able to go back there and perform and even happier when several of the nuns said they remembered me.

Our last show of the year was at the Valley City Fair in rural Medina County. A family named Mack had a pony farm there. For years, the Mack children earned college money taking ponies to county fairs for little ones to ride. Any colts that accompanied their mothers on these junkets drew even more interest. The Zoo Wagon ponies were always on loan from the Mack farm.

This last performance day was a beautiful one and we were all in good spirits. Margie came and Tom Byrne brought his lovely red-haired daughter to see the fair. Several days later the 8 year old was stricken with polio and severely handicapped by that ravaging disease. The post war period was plagued by polio until the Salk vaccine brought first relief. It came too late to help Tom's little girl, and whenever I look back on that day, I feel saddened as I remember how her running and skipping days were over.

The following year, the zoo director was hesitant to send the wagon out because Smoky and I were no longer available. Expecting to see Smoky the crowds that year were even larger. We had drawn over 100,000 in 10 weeks. Some kids followed her to many playgrounds enjoying her antics a dozen times. Clearly Smoky was THE star.

CHAPTER 10

HOLLYWOOD

Margie and I were busy planning our wedding. We set the date for September 28, 1946. Our huge parish had a six-month waiting list even though there were two weddings performed every Saturday. We had a beautiful wedding at St. Ignatius, where both of us had attended grade school. Soon after the wedding, we went shopping for a car.

We found a beautiful, pearl white 1940 Packard Super 8, 160, with nickel-plated radiator and bumpers and only 36,000 miles on the odometer. The four-door was on a used car lot and was listed at $1,638. Because it was a heavy gas user, it had been stored during the war. Margie's dad, George H. Roberts, a master radio repairman, did all of his own car's mechanical work, including engine overhauls. After critically examining this behemoth, he said, "Bill, buy this car immediately." We did. I didn't have a job at the time so Margie, who had a good job at the Veterans Administration, signed for the car.

Dog World, the magazine for breeders, carried a classified ad placed by Rennie Renfro, owner of the Hollywood dog, Daisy, star of the "Blondie" movies. Renfro was looking for people to train and work dogs for motion pictures. This was a job made to order for me.

I called Hollywood and learned that Rennie was on location in the California Mountains. Maddie, his wife, suggested that I just come on out. Margie and I decided to make this our wedding trip. I had little driving experience, especially on the right side of the road American-style, so I was somewhat apprehensive about motoring all the way across country. My only experience on the road had been driving jeeps and weapons carriers—not quite the same as maneuvering in civilian traffic. Because there were so many servicemen returning every day, the State of Ohio was issuing them driver's licenses without any tests. I have never read anywhere that this practice produced any increase in accidents. Jack Lewis, now discharged from the Coast Guard, decided to try his luck in California and offered to share the driving.

We started out in early October with Jack and I driving alternately. One day during my shift, we were caught in some heavy rain and Jack, who was resting on the back seat suddenly announced, "Bill, the roof leaks."

"That's impossible," I insisted.

"Look," he said, "the upholstery is wet on both sides under the windows."

I stopped the car and we checked under the rear fender wells. We saw that the metal had rusted away, leaving a six-inch hole high up in the fenders. A closer examination revealed that the fender beading had been cleverly doctored. A first-class paint job had concealed the patchwork. To make matters worse, we were driving on Texas red clay and this leakage permanently stained the handsome light-gray upholstery. I was very upset.

The dealer who sold us our car had told us that, for $200 under the table, he could get us a new Studebaker. We refused, so No Guts, as I would later christen our heap, was our only transportation, whether we liked it or not. The car had a slow pick-up, but after 50 m.p.h. it was all power. That straight-eight engine could really push that big car at higher speeds.

On Route 66, near Amarillo, I was driving and Jack, Margie and Smoky were all in the front seat. Once again we had encountered a downpour and Jack warned me, "Bill, don't let the car slide onto the muddy shoulder."

So I began watching the line along the edge of the highway instead of the road in front of me, and, sure enough, the car drifted off the road and hit the soft shoulder. I over corrected the skid and we flew back onto the highway, spinning backwards. The car did a couple of complete circles across the on-coming lane and we landed in a ditch heading in the right direction but on the wrong side of the road. The episode had seemed to go on endlessly. Steam was coming from everywhere and grass was growing on the hood, fenders and windshield.

I got out and walked around the car, checking for damage and noticed some mud pressed against my left rear fender. "Aw, gee," I complained, "I dented my fender."

Jack leaped out of the car yelling, "I've been through the war. I've survived kamikaze attacks and this is the closest I've ever been to getting killed! And he says, 'Aw, gee, I dented my fender.' #*A%+#/!!"

While Jack stormed, I laughed, and this made him even madder.

"I'm going to find a tractor to pull us out," he shouted back to us as he walked briskly up the highway. By that time I was realizing how lucky we had been not to meet any oncoming traffic during the skid. More good luck with Smoky, our mascot.

About a half hour later. Jack reappeared, standing behind the driver on a huge tractor. "It'll cost you 15 bucks," he yelled. "He wouldn't come out for less."

Gas was averaging 26 cents a gallon then, so $15 was a lot of money. A heavy chain was attached to the rear axle and No Guts was lifted out of the water-filled ditch and set back on the road.

Jack drove through the mountains, past Indigo, and, late into the night a peculiar whine began to sound from under the car. It grew louder. We were approaching Blythe, California, and decided to stop there for the night. We pulled into a garage parking lot at 3:15 a.m. and slept in the car until the garage opened.

The bad news was that the differential ring and pinion gear had to be replaced. Worse yet, the parts had to come by Greyhound from Los Angeles. We were marooned in the desert. We registered at the only motel and waited two days for the parts to arrive.

When they did come, they were the wrong size. The shop was able to machine a shim for the new ring, which was about 1/4 inch too thin. Another day lost and the job was still not finished.

The people who owned the motel offered Margie and me a job managing their place for $150 a week, fabulous pay for that time. Their previous manager had quit and they had had to come out to Blythe to oversee the property. They also owned the Hotel Stanley, located near Hollywood and Vine, and were eager to get back there. They knew I was hoping to get into motion picture work and they sweetened the deal by promising that, once a month, they would relieve us and that we could spend the weekend at the Stanley. All these incentives sounded good, but we just didn't want to stay out in the middle of the desert, so we turned them down.

They were kind enough to tell us that we could stay at the Stanley when we got to Hollywood. For the first five days we could rent a room at rent-control rates. After that we would be considered residents and the rent would have to be lowered. They already had all the full-time residents they could handle and could not promise us that status. Jack agreed to stay behind with the car and then drive on to meet us.

We boarded the bus to Los Angeles at 2 a.m. and had to sit right behind the driver. About an hour into the trip, I opened the zipper on Smoky's bag and caught her hair in it, and she let out a yelp. I had to admit to the angry driver that I had brought a dog on the bus. "No animals are allowed on buses and I should make you get off here and now. If we weren't in the desert, I would do just that!" he scolded. No more was said by either of us. We have traveled on planes, trains, buses and streetcars and no one ever had even an suspicion of Smoky's presence. She cried out just that once, when we were sitting right behind the Greyhound driver.

We arrived at the Stanley and registered. Jack arrived the next day and was assigned a room in the hotel annex. The latest bad news was that the rear end had gone out again. We piled into the car and clanked along with a godawful noise until we reached the LaBrea Packard dealership. This time we needed the works. Ring and pinion gears, spider gears, drive shaft, two universal joints and differential housing and bearings. The total came to $137. That, added to the $150 for the Blythe repairs, would have left us completely broke. I told the manager that I had a $100 refund coming from a deposit I had put on a Jeep back home. We must have looked pretty discouraged because he said, "You seem like a couple of nice kids. I'm going to release the car." It was a real break for us and we were grateful.

Among the rather unusual characters we met at the hotel was an Indian actor, who was known as Chief Stanley because he had played so many Indian chiefs in westerns. We also got to know the wrestler, Man Mountain Dean. The Chief offered to take us around to some movie studios and to act as our agent. Eagle Lion studios was just getting started and their office was filled with unknowns like us. Out on the lot, they were filming Big Red, a story about a horse. I explained what we could do to the casting director and he asked, "Are you selling yourself or the dog?"

"The dog," I answered. He had no part for Smoky and I didn't have enough confidence to try out for a people part, so we left. After that disappointing effort, the Chief gave up on us.

I called the Rennie Renfro Kennel. Neal Gazely, Rennie's head trainer and kennel manager, invited me out, but reminded me that Rennie was still on location. Neal was a soft-spoken man and a dapper dresser. I liked him immediately. The California sun had aged his fair skin, so he looked older than his 34 years.

I had Smoky do some of her tricks and some routines we had seen in the movies. He was quite impressed but was straightforward with me and said, "Look, Bill, I can't hire you without Rennie's okay, but if you'll come out and work with some other dogs, I'll find you as much studio work as I can."

He told me that Rennie had two other handlers working for him, James (Jimmy) Jack and a fellow named Schreiber, who lived with his family in a motor home on the property. Schreiber was about to leave for other employment.

Rennie Renfro had been a world champion diver. He was known for jumping from a 100-foot-high platform into a tank of water five feet deep. After his diving career was over, he became a movie stunt man. He once refused to do a stunt requiring him to ride a motorcycle around a curve and over a cliff. A parachute would be used to break the fall. Rennie said there wasn't enough altitude to allow a parachute to open. The stunt woman who agreed to try it was killed.

An Italian dog trainer had had some success with Barkies (short subject films), in which dogs wore people clothes and walked around on their hind legs imitating humans in cops and robbers comedies. The Italian returned to his home in Europe and Rennie took over his dog business.

His kennel had about 70 dogs. Daisy and the pups were Rennie's top dogs and worked regularly for Columbia Pictures in the "Blondie" series. Some of his other dogs included, Hobo, General, a Great Dane who worked with Red Skelton and an old hound dog that had been used in several films. These dogs had been trained to perform. Others were what they called atmosphere dogs, dogs that walked around in the background in movie scenes.

I started by training a nice mongrel named Butch, a $5 dollar pound dog. Many of the best dogs in motion pictures came from the pound. Butch was a thinking dog, the type that tries to outsmart the trainer. You need good instincts to handle that kind. Much like Smoky, Butch could baffle you by acting like he didn't get things when he understood everything perfectly. He learned quickly and I soon had him in control. He liked all the physical work I could give him and enjoyed scaling an eight-foot wall on command. Gazely was on to Butch, too, so we had no problems with this fine dog.

Next, I was assigned to train an English Setter. This dog couldn't let a sparrow pass by without going into a point. He was a nice dog, but he was untrainable for motion pictures. He understood what I was trying to teach him, but was easily distracted by any birds in the area and could not maintain continuity in his performance. In his kennel, he spent all day pacing the concrete, freezing in mid step as he set his point every time he spotted a bird. He worked so hard he was too thin and we couldn't keep his weight up even with a special vet diet. Setters and pointers are needed in films, but too few can be trained beyond the specialty for which they are bred.

The top dogs in the movies receive royal treatment just like their human counterparts. Concessions are made. Great animals like Lassie and Benji will be given extra leeway such as allowing the handler to talk out loud to the dog and then later cutting the voice from the sound track. Other times, voices are dubbed in. The directors are willing to shoot all the takes they need and, if a routine doesn't work, they will try something else. A star dog gets full attention when it is his movie, a movie like "Lassie Come Home."

A trained dog in a "people movie" is expected to come on the set prepared to fit in and do the things he was trained to do without slowing down production and running up costs. These dogs respond quickly to hand signals and commands.

Occasionally, there is some jealousy on the part of supporting actors because of the good money some of the animal stars make. In some cases, there is an outright hatred of movie dogs on the part of behind-the-scenes workers. Once, I was summoned with "Hey, doggie!" by one of these people. An atmosphere dog was paid $15 a day, a working dog, $25. Contract dogs like Lassie made $1,000 a week. Daisy earned $500 a week when working. Their handlers made more than $125 a day.

Many actors do not want to be in scenes with animals or children because they are such scene stealers. But everyone, animal or human, contributes to the success of a movie and should be appreciated. The more successful the film, the more work there is for all. In the 1920s, Rin Tin Tin's movies saved Warner Brothers Studios and became a legend in the film industry.

The best dog trainers, I think, match the training methods to the personality of the dog and apply just the right amount of pressure. Like athletes, certain dogs are aggressive and others, equally intelligent, are more laid back. You control or master the dominant ones. You encourage the reticent ones with enthusiasm. Of course, you must encourage the strong-minded ones also. You cannot handle all dogs the same way. This is true of children as well. So often, teachers use the same techniques on all children, expecting similar results. Animal trainers, coaches and teachers who excel have a gift. They know who has potential and how to develop it. They ride hard on some and gently encourage others.

We once performed at Thompson Ramo Waldridge (TRW), whose headquarters were in Cleveland. Another speaker on the program was Bob Voights, an assistant coach with the Cleveland Browns. He had just accepted a head coaching position at Northwestern University. When I mentioned to him that dog training is a lot like coaching, he reacted with horror and I can still see that expression on his face. But, doesn't a football coach squat down like a lineman to demonstrate the proper stance? And doesn't he adjust that stance to just the right arch to show how to make a block on an opposing lineman? A coach teaches the basics according to his own style and much of the coach's personality, drive and encouragement become part of the student's make-up.

Corrections will be made in technique as the player moves from boyhood to high school to college. Even as a pro, when a player changes teams, his training will be adjusted to the new coaching philosophy. Paul Brown's coaching techniques revolutionized professional football after World War II, and his disciples have been extremely successful over the years. As many as 40 coaches and assistant coaches, Brown's proteges, have worked in professional and college football at the same time. This is a perfect example of the positive influence of a great teacher.

We had to move from the Stanley to a place in Studio City. The family that owned the house had rented out every spare bedroom for $125 a month. It was a share-the-kitchen deal. After only a week, Margie couldn't stand it any longer, so we moved again. We were hoping a cottage at Rennie's place would become available.

To start me working in films, Neal called Henry East, a successful trainer whose most famous pupil was Asta, the Wire-haired Terrier of the "Thin Man" series which starred William Powell and Myrna Loy. Henry took me to MGM to help with a new Asta. Wirehairs have a lower than average training capability, although, as a breed, they are sweet dogs. The original Asta had died and it took four Wirehairs, colored alike, to accomplish what their predecessor had done.

Different breeds have different levels of trainability. When a breeder is set on developing a color, such as the red in an Irish Setter or Irish Terrier, the results often produce fewer trainable dogs. Working dogs like Shepherds and Dobermans are bred to interact with a handler and easily obey commands.

One of the worst things that can happen to a breed, with reference to trainability, is breeding to establish a color or to produce dominant markings. This is often done by inbreeding to double up the genes, but this not only doubles the desirable genes but the undesirable ones as well. Thus, you can develop nervous, high-strung, difficult dogs right along with the good trainable ones. To the credit of the most dedicated breeders, who are determined to maintain high standards, all pure-bred dogs have improved greatly.

Another negative thing that can happen is for a breed to take off in popularity. Fly-by-night breeders skim off the profits and take little responsibility for the quality of their dogs. The careful breeders make little, if any, real money in the game. The costs for professional handlers to show their dogs, the high prices of breeding stock, the kennel maintenance expenses and the veterinarian bills make breeding more of a hobby than a get-rich-quick business. Sometimes movie dogs have hurt their breeds. Rin Tin Tin's fame caused the rapid growth in the demand for German Shepherds. My Own Brucie, a top show Cocker Spaniel, helped cause the cocker population explosion.

Neal Gazely had worked out the training probabilities according to breed. Out of 24 randomly picked Collies, only three would be highly trainable. Collies were bred more for nose, color and markings. When you located a great one, there was no limit to what you could do with him. Lassie was a case in point.

In Neal's mind, German Shepherds could produce seven out of ten great dogs. For Wire-haired Terriers, he figured only one out of 25. Golden Retrievers and Labradors were responsive and Poodles were very good. Hunting dogs were even better in their own specialties and mixed-breeds were high-percentage trainable. In all cases, the dog must be very carefully selected by an expert eye.

The kennel received a call for a dog act to perform with talented children hopeful of establishing movie careers. Neal threw the engagement to Smoky and me and we appeared at a downtown Los Angeles auditorium. It was a fast moving show of dancers, singers and speciality acts ages ranging from 5 to 16. The kids were all good, performing for some movie scouts in the audience.

The first movie I worked with Henry East was a Doctor Gillespie picture starring Lionel and Ethel Barrymore, Gig Young and Lucille Bremer. Henry's main Wire-hair was smart enough to handle the whole part, but was somewhat wooden. (Maybe he had been overtrained.) So they used another Wire-hair who was very cute and intelligent-looking in close-ups, but untrainable for action shots.

Another was used in running scenes because the main dog moved slowly and mechanically. We hated to turn the running dog loose because we always had a heck of a time rounding him up. All the dogs were made up to look alike. Henry's chief kennel trainer was Sam Williamson, who had been a Florida Greyhound trainer for the dog races. Sam became very successful at training other movie dogs.

We were summoned one day to RKO where they were filming "Magic Town," starring Jimmy Stewart and Jane Wyman. Pev Marley was the cameraman and we spent our down time talking about dogs. Rudd Weatherwax, Lassie's famous trainer, had a dog on the set in a bit part. The dog bit Stewart. Rudd and the dog had been kicked off the lot. We would be shooting for just one day. In the scene, Stewart walks into town. Some kids are shooting baskets, so he steps up and tosses a couple with them. The dog jumps up and down to meet the ball. We did just fine, but the scene was cut from the movie.

I was invited to meet Rudd Weatherwax at his home in the San Fernando Valley, not far from Rennie's place. Rudd lived in a new ranch-style house with a five-foot-high cyclone fence encircling the front yard. He explained that Pal, who earned his fame as Lassie, was an incurable motorcycle chaser. To keep his valuable star from harm, he had the fence installed.

Rudd had a five-year dream contract. Pal earned $1,000 a week when he worked and $500 a week when he didn't. Rudd was viewed as THE master trainer by the other Hollywood handlers and, over the years, produced and trained many successive Lassies.

Having worked with him, Gazely had an enormous respect for Rudd. Weatherwax was patient to the utmost. Neal said that during training breaks, Rudd would make a lasso loop from a piece of kite string and tie it to a stick. Then he would sit motionless for long periods, dangling the lasso over a floor-level hole in the wall. When a mouse emerged, attracted by the dog kibbles placed enticingly outside his door, Rudd pulled up the lasso, capturing the wriggling animal.

Rudd had worked for Henry East and had trained the original Asta. He also worked at one time for Rennie Renfro and had trained the original Daisy. He was a Hollywood legend.

He was also quite a businessman. MGM studios once bought a dog and asked Rudd to train and handle it for a movie. When the movie was finished, the studio asked him to board the dog at his kennel. Much later, the studio heads brought in some cost-cutters who did not want to continue paying board for this dog. Rudd was asked if he wanted to buy the dog. He said no, because there were few calls for that particular breed. Then they asked if he would take the dog off their hands. Rudd said he would. Some time later, the studio needed that very type for another picture. Rudd not only negotiated a new contract for the dog, but collected the handling fees as well.

There were good years and bad years in the animal-training end of show business. Sometimes unforeseen circumstances could damage a man's career. Carl Spitz, the owner and talented trainer of Buck, the St. Bernard used in "Call of the Wild," was almost blackballed during the war because of his German background. He eked out a living boarding dogs and giving lessons in obedience training.

Frank Barnes, another old-timer in the business, worked with Lee Duncan to train the German Shepherd, Grey Shadow. Duncan was the World War I Army captain who had found the puppy, Rin Tin Tin, in a German trench. Barnes had earned fame and fortune by training Rin Tin Tin IV for an early television series.

I met Earl Johnson who worked with Roy Rogers' dog Bullitt. We all belonged to the Hollywood Animal Handlers and Trainers Association, which had just been formed.

At Rennie's kennel, Petey, a Siamese, was the only resident cat. Petey was a lovable cat with crossed eyes. If he caught you looking at him, he always gave you a great big MeeeOOOW! On a picture with Claude Raines, Petey and his handler were assigned a dressing room. It wasn't because Petey was such a big star. It was because Raines hated all cats and Petey in particular. When Raines looked at the cat and the cat responded with his usual friendly MeeeOOOW, the actor raged so loud he could be heard all over the set. The director decided to keep the cat out of sight between takes. Raines, fine actor that he was, never even hinted at his disdain for Petey during filming.

Rennie was currently handling Daisy. He yelled at the dog if he was slow getting the message. Part of this I'm sure was because of Rennie's hearing problem. The old Daisy was spirited and didn't cower, but the young Daisy was more timid and had to be handled more carefully. Another problem about using a mix-breed dog is that you never can find another that is an exact duplicate of the original star. You may also get a different personality, which requires a change in training technique. Daisy, a Poodle-Spaniel and a little something else, was difficult to match.

The five pups were toy white poodles, trimmed and dyed tan around they eyes and parts of their bodies to give them a zany look. The original Daisy pups were killed in a tragic accident at the studio. A gasoline-driven generator was parked near the station wagon they were sleeping in and they were asphyxiated by the carbon monoxide.

A trainer named Frank Inn had just left Rennie before I arrived and was now working for Rudd Weatherwax. Inn later owned and trained the wonderful dog, Benji. Rudd's brothers were also handlers and trainers.

When Rudd first struck out on his own, his former employers caused him great difficulty by blackballing him with the movie studios. With his house and car in hock, he struggled financially, but continued to train his Collie, Pal, who had been given to him in payment of a $10 debt. When "Lassie Come Home" was being cast, the studio sent a big, black limo to the various kennels to invite their dogs to audition. Pal was rejected with the rest, but Rudd kept up his training. Finally, unable to choose their star, the studio invited all the dogs back for another viewing. This time Pal was ready and got the job.

Rudd was knocked dead by Smoky's personality and watched me putting Smoky through her paces. He was in awe. "I'd be afraid to tackle a dog that small," he said. When I had her spell her name, he watched us both very carefully, trying to spot some cue from me. (In later years, Rudd did train a Yorkie and used some of our tricks.) Smoky was in the mood for the spelling and she was terrific. Because I force trained her, Smoky didn't always perform the spelling well.

Pal (Lassie) was a house dog, as were Asta and Daisy. Almost all the great dogs are house pets. Many field trial champions, show dogs, hunting dogs and search dogs do so well because of the ongoing encouragement, training and close companionship of their masters. The team is working together all the time. There is no substitute for the rapport established in such a relationship.

One difficulty for the house dog is that others members of the household can interfere with their discipline. Who is in control of the animal must be clearly established at the beginning to prevent difficulty. If children want to play with the dog and the dog recognizes the difference between work and play, then all will be well. But, if the dog uses the play to avoid discipline, then it must be hands off. It may be necessary to get a separate pet for the children. I once knew a seeing-eye dog who could be a family pet, rollicking and romping about with abandon, and, yet, in harness would be all business.

Henry East supplied the dog for Universal's "The Egg and I," with Fred MacMurray, Claudette Colbert and Louise Albritton. I worked with him in the scenes with the English Setter under the stove. This setter was a very nice one, working well under Henry's commands. The dairy farmer next to Rennie's land furnished the cows for the fair scenes.

At that time, Rennie had five dogs working simultaneously at Warner Brothers. Warner's wrote dogs into almost every movie because of their appreciation for Rin Tin Tin. I worked on "Deep Valley," directed by Jean Negulesco and starring Dane Clark, Ida Lupino, Wayne Morris, Fay Bainter and Henry Hull.

In this picture I handled Hobo, filling in for Neal. Then we did "Woman in White," starring Alexis Smith and Eleanor Parker. One thing Neal Gazely emphasized was not to let others tell you what to do with your dog. He cited a case where someone wanted a Great Dane to move faster in a scene and suggested putting turpentine on him. Because of such incidents, the ASPCA had agents on every set. During the filming, the studios paid the agents' salaries.

Rennie was still on location with Daisy and this was causing a problem for Columbia in filming the latest "Blondie" movie. These quickies, starring Penny Singleton and Arthur Lake, were favorites with the fans. The stars had to memorize as many lines in two weeks as their counterparts in the big movies learned in six months. During Daisy's absence, the pups had to fill in. I was the only handler currently available because all the other trainers were busy in productions elsewhere.

One of the standard scenes in the "Blondie" movies featured Dagwood, late for work as usual, running out the front door and colliding with the mailman, Mr. Beasley, sending both him and his letters flying into the air. Blondie, the kids and the dogs were lined up at the door and a big wind fan was blowing for the scattered-letters effect.

With Daisy unavailable, the director, Abbie Berlin decided to try a new wrinkle. He had seen the Daisy pup, Elmer, performing in Ken Murray's "Blackouts," a live vaudeville show. Rennie and the dogs were always a big hit. After the performance, Rennie ran off the stage with all the dogs except Elmer, who continued to sit on a table, applauding with his paws. Rennie ran back out, coaxing and pleading, while the pup stayed where he was, applauding. Finally, Rennie came out and pushed the table off stage with Elmer applauding all the way. This brought down the house.

Berlin wanted Elmer to wear a special little mail bag around his neck and to go outside through Daisy's front door flap. There he would meet the mailman and sit up to applaud. Mr. Beasley was to slip the mail into Elmer's bag and Elmer would come back in through the little door. It sounds easy, but poor Elmer knew only one trick, and wasn't willing to learn another. Neal advised Berlin to use Tick, the biggest of the pups. He wasn't as cute, but was well trained and could do the part. No deal. The director wanted Elmer and that was that.

Take One: I lined up the dogs in their sit-up position. Blondie was holding Dagwood's coffee, the kids were near the door and Bumstead was about to begin his run. The fan was started and whoosh! The littlest pup, near the wind machine, was picked up and blown out the door, past the other pups. They watched him roll by and then followed him outside.

Take Two: I set the dogs down once again, away from the fan and nearer the front door. This time it worked.

Once, when the Bumstead house was used on another picture, the flap was nailed shut to keep it from opening on a windy day. When the house came back for use in the next "Blondie" picture, everyone had forgotten about the flap. Daisy came running down the stairs and, as usual, hit the flap with his head and bounced back several feet. The poor little guy was stunned.

In the movie we were shooting, Elmer was going to solve Dagwood's collision problem and be the hero of the day. But that flap caused trouble for Elmer, too. He was supposed to go through the little door, carrying his mail bag. When the timid dog started through, the flap swung back and popped him gently on the head. He refused to try again. We tied dark fishing line to his collar and I pulled him through the flap. Then he ambled down the walk, sat up and applauded for Mr. Beasley, took the letter the mailman gave him and had to be towed back through the flap. End of scene.

Most studios had spider boxes that distributed power from outdoor generators for the lighting on the sets. These boxes were open on the sides, exposing the high voltage equipment inside. Trainers made sure none of the male dogs lifted his leg in the vicinity of the boxes, lest the poor fellow be electrocuted.

Smoky and I continued our stage work at the Hollywood Canteen. It was still in operation, although the big stars who had visited during the war did not come by anymore. A lot of GIs still used the recreational facilities. I volunteered and our act was scheduled.

At the canteen, I got to know the backstage manager, an elderly gentleman called Pop. It wasn't easy! This guy had seen it all and was totally unimpressed by anything. He just sat with his feet propped up on another chair and read his paperbacks. His gruff manner never changed as the acts filed on and off stage.

I carried Smoky onto the stage in her little bag, delivering my patter and surprising the audience with the little dog's appearance. When I set her down, instead of weaving in and out through my legs, Smoky took off and was running around the stage curtains, something she had never done before. I started looking for her and, as I was looking, she came out, spotted me and darted behind the curtains again. The pianist was playing "Pretty Baby" and the audience was starting to howl.

Every time I came out of one curtain, she disappeared behind another. When I was behind the curtains calling for her, she was prancing around on the stage, playing to the audience. I composed myself and we finished our act in front of a very lively audience. I glanced backstage and there was Pop, standing up, his book cast aside, laughing and clapping harder than anyone else. He shook my hand and told me we had a great act. Smoky had become one of the big stars of the Hollywood Canteen.

A request came to Rennie's for a special private show to be given at the home of producer Milton Sperling. I took Smoky and the equipment to his home near Hollywood and gave a show for five small children. I always enjoyed performing for children, and these little ones loved the show.

Soon after that, Rennie Renfro returned home for a brief visit before going lion hunting in the mountains. He was a short man with bright blue eyes, a genial smile and gray hair. He had a fast-moving gait that belied his 50-plus years. We met in the training building that we used in bad weather. Neal introduced me, "Bill here has trained only one dog, but she is a heck of a dog."

Rennie had me put Smoky through some other paces. Then he asked me to have her stay with him. In this routine the dog stays with a stranger as though they were companions. Smoky stuck to Rennie like glue. No matter how he tried to shake her with sudden reverses and turns, she was right there.

"Neal!" Rennie shouted, "this dog is better trained than anything we have in our kennel!"

But I could not get Rennie's commitment for a guaranteed minimum salary. He had had several bad experiences with trainers who hadn't worked out and he wasn't about to have it happen again. Neal was as disappointed as I was and continued to throw every job he could find my way.

It was no use, though. Margie was ill. She hated being alone from 7 a.m. to 10 p.m. every day. The studio policy was to stretch days rather than to schedule extra ones. It was cheaper. Margie hated Hollywood. She wasn't eating. She hated the housing arrangements. They were substandard and expensive. We talked it over and decided it might be best for her to go back home. I could stay in a small cabin on Rennie's ranch and cut my expenses while I continued establishing my credentials, hoping for a steady income. We had been married only three months, and this was a lousy life style.

Her job with the VA was waiting. She had been offered a job with the VA in Los Angeles, but had no way to get back and forth to work. We could not afford a second car. It was hopeless. Reluctantly we made our way to the train station and said our sad good-byes. Once again we would be separated.

Sadly Margie boarded the Union Pacific, promising to return if I could get a contract. I had applied for a job as a flight photographer at the National Advisory Committee for Aeronautics (NACA) in Cleveland. (The NACA became NASA in 1957.) If that job materialized, I told Margie, I would come back to Ohio.

I moved into the cabin. It was unheated and had no cooking range or refrigerator. The trainer who was planning to leave was still living there. The living conditions were unpleasant, to say the least. I looked at Smoky, stooped down and patted her, thinking, given our experience with two years in tents, jungles, coral reefs, tropical storms, just less than a year before, it wasn't bad.

Several days later, I received a letter from Margie telling me that she was pregnant. Now I understood why she had been so sick. She was living with her parents and back to work, so she considered our situation to be bearable, at least for a while.

Smoky was invited to entertain at the TRW Southern California Plant Christmas show. Our act had been recommended by TRW's Cleveland Headquarters. Here too was a large appreciative audience.

Warner Brothers was making the movie "Night Unto Night" and asked to look at some dogs for a part that was being written into the script in the middle of the picture. Neal had me take in Butch, the brown-and-white mongrel I had been training. Don Siegel, the director, and Owen Krump, the producer, both liked the dog, so we started the next day.

With our dogs working in five pictures, we were really busy. Not all days were shooting days for our dogs and handlers might be working with different dogs on different days. This was my first picture. It was also Don

Siegel's first as a director and Viveca Lindfors first American film. The male star was Ronald Reagan, a contract actor at Warner Brothers.

On the set, there is a lot of down time, but I was interested in everything from a photographer's point of view. It was fascinating to watch the lighting experts and cameramen working on the placement of their equipment.

The set featured a beach scene. The crew mounted a 100-foot-long clear plastic sheet on rollers five feet apart, one higher than the other. The sheet was painted with random black streaks and was rolled up and down by a slow-turning motor. When backlighted in the darkened sound stage, it produced the effect of waves shimmering in the moonlight. The moon was a round light placed high up, behind a screen. With the sand on the fake beach, the result was surprisingly realistic.

In this scene, as Reagan was walking with his dog on the beach, he was to experience an epileptic seizure and fall to the sand. Instead of filming the changing expressions on the actor's face, the director had decided to make the dog the center of the action. The camera would move to Reagan's hand writhing in the sand as the dog moved in out of curiosity. For these close-ups, a second unit headed by Jimmy Leicester, a skilled cameraman, was called in. A team of four worked on the details of this extremely close camera work.

We went to another sound stage to work in private. An extra was brought along to do the writhing hand. Butch was to act curious at first. (This part was easy. A good dog is always curious.) Then he was to sniff the hand and then attack it. Actually, by this time the hand was gone and we were working on a close-up of the dog's face. Now we had some problems. Butch was so friendly, I couldn't get him to attack. I discovered that, for some reason, if I put a coat over my head, he became enraged and lunged at me. The minute I called out my name and uncovered my head, he was as loving as ever.

The lunging was great, but he did it so fast, the camera could not record enough footage. We needed some restraint. We decided to drive two nails into the floor, one on each side of the dog. Then we would attach copper wires to his collar and fasten the wires to the nails. This would keep the dog at a given distance, allowing the camera to record his violent reaction. The wires needed to be stained with iodine so they would not be picked up by the camera. We had everything planned perfectly. And then, we waited.

The carpenters' union said no one but a carpenter could pound the nails into the floor. If we used any wire, an electrician had to install it. It would take two electricians to do the job—one to attach the wires and one on each side to snip the dog loose. A prop man had to color the wires with the iodine. We waited half a day for these people to arrive.

We finally began shooting the sequence. Butch was terrific. He did everything right. In the attacking scene, the restraining wires gave Leicester plenty of footage of an enraged, snarling, charging dog. The head was shown full-size on the theater screen. The next day's script called for the dog to reverse his attitude, place his tail between his legs and run off, kiyipping. Fade out.

There was no way this dog was going to back off. Leicester said he could dub in the sound of the kiyipping, fading out the sound as the dog ran away. I tied Butch's tail between his legs with brown thread, and the prop man agreed to get under the coat only if the released dog would run the other way. As his handler, I had to be the one to call him off the attack, standing behind Butch and off to the side.

The attack began. After a few moments, the wires were cut and Butch lunged forward. The prop man threw off the coat and I called the dog. He turned immediately, running away from the camera with his tail between his legs. End of scene. I saw "Night Unto Night" several years later, and the whole scene was used in the picture.

I was returning to my car one evening and I saw the producer's wife calling her husband over to see the cute little dog standing on the back of the driver's seat. I told them it was my dog. I shared some of her story with them and had her run through a few simple tricks. Mrs. Krump said, "Oh, Owen, why don't you write this dog into this picture?"

He replied, "This dog is worth too much to be in this picture. We'll put her in my next picture!"

It was an exciting prospect, but I was feeling a little guilty. I was on the lot because I was working for Rennie, not for myself. But, I had to have Smoky with me at all times. I often remembered this pleasant encounter, but I never pursued the offer. This probably was the turning point of our motion picture career. That crossroad one meets and a selection of pursuit of life's work hangs in balance. The Krumps were happily impressed and dead serious with their suggestion.

There was another scene that Butch worked in with Reagan and Lindfors. It was a simple scene with Reagan knocking on a door and

Lindfors opening the door and leaning down to pet Butch. The three of us had long dog conversations between takes.

"Night Unto Night" was kept under wraps for two years before it was released. It was not considered to be a great film, but it pioneered in dealing with the subject of mental and physical disorders. In general, the studios avoided those subjects like the plague. Warner's showed admirable courage. It was a unique idea on the part of the director to show a sensitive scene through the emotions of a dog, and I am proud to have handled that dog.

Christmas and New Year's Day had passed with no word from Rennie. He promised to mention our act to Ken Murray. If Murray was interested. Smoky and I might be able to fill in for Rennie and his dogs from time to time. Nothing ever materialized. Rennie and Murray played cards weekly with Billy Gilbert and Ben Turpin.

Rennie had a tame gorilla that he sometimes used in pictures. As a gag, he once put the gorilla in the closet Turpin always used to hang his hat. That night, when Turpin opened the closet door, he was so shocked that, his friends said his eyes uncrossed. Turpin, famous for his severely cross-eyed look, was not amused. He walked out, called his insurance company and took out a $50,000 policy on his eyes.

Margie called to tell me that I had gotten a telegram from the Cleveland NACA informing me of a job opening as a flight photographer. Margie had called the air lab to tell them that I was in California. They said they could hold the job for just one week because the program was ready to roll and they needed someone right away. The work involved research on icing in flight. The job would pay $3,000 to $5,000 a year. If I could report on Monday, the 28th of January, 1947, the job was mine.

I was just about broke. The studio work had been too sparse to pay for anything but food and gas. My mother called to urge me to come home. After all, Margie was expecting and I had no solid prospects in California. She had planned to give us silverware as a wedding present, but six months had passed and the department store was still unable to deliver the order. She got a refund of $70 and wired it to me. I would go home.

Goldie had made arrangements for me to meet Indy Rice, a well-known breeder of Yorkies who lived in Los Angeles. The Rices had a very successful oriental rug business. They also had an apartment full of Yorkies, splendid specimens. Several of them were owned by movie stars and Indy was taking care of them. Among the lot were several one-pounders, each about four inches high. Indy wanted me to meet another breeder from Corona del Mar, but I told her I just had to get back to Ohio. Too bad I didn't meet Indy sooner. She was a personal friend of Jack Warner.

She telephoned her friend, Kay Finch, a talented ceramist and Yorkie breeder. Indy told me Kay's ceramic work had begun with an eight-dollar kiln which she turned into a $100,000-a-year business in five years. Her animal figures were in gift shops and department stores all over the country. We had a long talk on the phone and Kay wanted very much for Smoky and me to come to Corona del Mar, but it was impossible. I had to leave a couple of days early so that, if I had car trouble, I could still make the deadline. Kay sent us some beautiful ceramics, including a life-size one of "Puddin," a Yorkie that was a one-of-a-kind color experiment. It was truly chocolate pudding colored. Underneath the glaze, Kay wrote, "For Smoky from Kay, 1947."

For many years, Kay remained a dominant figure in the dog world. She also bred Afghans and one others was judged Best in Show at the prestigious Westminster Dog Show in New York. Later, she became a prominent dog show judge herself.

Neal Gazely was desperate to keep me. He pleaded with me to stay and gave me Rudd Weatherwax's agent's name and phone number. Up to that time, Rudd was the only motion picture dog owner to have his own agent. I explained that I needed a commitment and Rennie hadn't offered me one.

When Jimmy Vaugh, the kennel man, heard that I was going back east, he asked to go along. His future with Rennie wasn't looking any too bright, either. He packed up a small bag and said he would take the Greyhound from Cleveland to New York, his destination. He didn't know how to drive, so I would have companionship on the trip, but no relief.

The most memorable part of the trip was while driving into a Kansas town at two o'clock one morning, I made a wrong turn on a poorly marked highway and we got lost. We stopped to check the map. Suddenly, the car was surrounded by eight men with pistols and rifles and one of them started hammering on the window. Vaugh was dragged out, slammed against the car and searched. I was asked to produce the car's title, which I did. They demanded to know where we were going and where we had come from. I explained that we had made a wrong turn and were checking the map to find our way back.

I got out Smoky's scrap book and showed it to their leader, pointing to the little dog on the seat. He looked at the newspaper clippings, studied

Smoky closely and finally pronounced us "okay." He called off his posse. I asked what the heck was going on. "Someone just pulled a big robbery and got away in a car that matches yours," he said. He told us how to get back on the right road and we got out of there fast, happy to have our skin intact.

The next night, outside Indianapolis, a heavy fog began to lay down. At first, the car's top was just under it, but then it settled down over us until we could see almost nothing. On the four-lane divided highway, I could just make out the center line. I stayed right on it, ready to make adjustments should something suddenly appear in front of me.

For many miles, I never saw another car or truck. Vaugh slept all night in the back seat, but if you want real company while on a lonely, intense drive, a great companion dog will wake up beside you and after checking things out nuzzle up giving you a big lick in the face. It happens often enough to keep up your spirits. It was a routine of her own in which my pal Smoky excelled in years of our traveling alone to nightclubs and theaters.

We arrived in the Cleveland area on Saturday morning. The streets were clear. I dropped Jim Vaugh off at the Greyhound station downtown and headed out to the west side. This last leg had been an exhausting 30-hour drive. I was very happy to be home.

CHAPTER 11

SHOW BUSINESS AND FLIGHT RESEARCH

The personnel manager took me to the photo lab. The younger employees were all ex-servicemen, so it was something like being in the military again. My job was to fly as a photographer with research crews on flight-icing missions in WWII B-24 Liberator and B-25 Mitchell bombers.

Cleveland NACA was the Flight Propulsion Center, doing research on reciprocating engines, jet engines and rockets. The center was also interested in other fields of development, including fuels and lubricants, air foils, sub and supersonic tunnel experiments and other potential aeronautical problems. The National Advisory Committee for Aeronautics was founded in 1916 at Langley Field in Virginia to assist in aeronautic research. Because of the huge costs and limited manpower, private industry did not undertake much aviation development. NACA was in the forefront of development after 1916, and it was the agency from which the National Aeronautical and Space Agency (NASA) developed.

Lewis Rodert, a scientist from Langley, later Ames Research Lab in California and then Cleveland, had developed a de-icing system for aircraft. It was tested at Ames on a Commando C-46, and now the problems encountered under actual flight conditions were to be resolved in three locations over the next three years. Cleveland was the most ideal location for flight-icing research, because the Great Lakes weather frequently set up the right flying conditions for it.

The B-24 and B-25 had elaborate anti-icing and de-icing equipment and were the most de-icible planes in the world. Lew Rodert's machine was like a compact hot-air furnace with air ducts to the leading edges of the plane's wings and tail fins. By brute force, it could melt off the worst icing that formed on the wings.

The first flight was the next morning, January 29, 1947. At the plane, I was introduced to Chief Test Pilot William (Eb) Gough, a former Navy lieutenant commander who flew PBYs in the far Pacific, and co-pilot Howard Lily. The predawn weather was horrible and all aircraft had been grounded. It was just right for our mission.

Taking off in heavy wind gusts, we began the roughest ride I had ever experienced. At least we were over friendly territory, no planes to shoot us down, no ack-ack to puncture our fuselage, no enemy to capture us if we had to bail out and no thousands of miles of ocean to swim. Although we carried parachutes, the Lake Erie winter temperatures made the potential of survival short term at best.

We found ice and it found us.

During this first mission, we landed at the Traverse City, Michigan, Coast Guard Station, hoping the accumulated ice hadn't melted so we could get some good pictures. It hadn't and we did.

The takeoff was something else. Gough taxied to the end of the runway and slid off the icy turnaround pad. A couple of prop bursts pulled us back onto the pad. We revved up and roared from side to side down the runway, fishtailing on the ice. Gough and Lilly maneuvered somehow to keep the tail from pulling up even with the nose. Finally, we lifted off the ground and continued our adventurous flight.

We flew home in an inky blackness. When we made a pass at the Cleveland airstrip, we suddenly saw the Bomber Plant (now the IX Center) looming off our port wing. We pulled up and instead headed for Columbus, where the field was clear.

While we waited at the airstrip there for a ride to town, the pilot Eb Gough, walked up to me, his helmet, earphones and throat mike still in place, and asked, "Bill, how many kids do you have?"

"One on the way," I boasted.

"Well," he said, "500 feet of that runway was for your kid." Gough explained he allocated 500' for each child of all crewmen. "That's why we're here in Columbus."

I loved that guy from that moment on. He was always a hero to me. I found out later that he had been a hero in the Navy, too. (PBY: The Catalina Flying Boat. By Rosco Creed, Naval Institute Press, 1985.)

The next day the weather was so bad, we had to take a train back to Cleveland.

Through booking agents, Smoky and I began playing in night clubs, theaters and a few shows in odd places like ice hockey games and between bouts in boxing rings. Usually, there were a number of other acts playing with us. The hockey management invited us back to make solo appearances. For these shows they put a big sheet of plywood over the ice to give Smoky better footing. The pipe organ, used as a background for recreational skating, pumped out our music. Three big spotlights, shining down from the rafters, tracked our every movement. We were always a smash and the full house applauded long and hard.

Theatrical booking agents were often characters right out of a Damon Runyan story. Leo Fredericks, a pleasant, soft-spoken, balding man, with elastic garters on his sleeves, opened shirt and loosened tie, always sat at his lonely post in a dark, otherwise barren room. A single light bulb, hanging from the ceiling on a wire, illuminated his old flat-top desk. He passed his time peering through wire-rimmed glasses at the Racing Form. Leo's wife was a stripper turned seamstress, who was famous for the costumes she designed for burlesque. Leo preferred that I use a table in our act, because people in the back rows might not be able to see Smoky working on the floor. However, I knew that, if they couldn't see the dog, customers in the back just stood up.

The Sennes brothers were big booking agents who sent talent to theaters and top clubs all over the country. They usually booked acts that were in the business full time and the jobs often lasted for weeks at a time, which didn't interest me. Time with my family was more important. After two years of tenting from Australia to Korea, I appreciated family life. I did a couple of dates for the Sennes.

Sid Freeman was doing a lot of booking, but at the lowest possible rates. He liked package deals and chauffeured the acts around for weekend dates in Ohio and Pennsylvania. Some of Sid's acts were topnotch. Among those who accepted bookings to supplement their regular income were Smiley and Sue, a country comedy act. In pre "Hee-Haw" style, Smiley cracked jokes while Sue strummed her guitar and sang. We traveled with a number of fine musicians who picked up weekend gigs when they were between road shows.

A tap dancer from Detroit, who danced with calves' ankles grafted onto his ankles in infancy because of a birth defect was probably the most unusual act I ever saw. He was written up in "Ripley's Believe It Or Not." The Boucairs, an adagio team from France, were nearing the end of their long worldwide career. Les Boucair opened a Citroen auto dealership, and they ran a dance studio together. Their act was first rate and very strenuous. It reached its climax as he threw his wife over his shoulder, allowing her to plunge head-first toward the floor. He caught her just an inch before she hit. The more you watched them, the scarier it got, and the crowd always gasped. It was great theater.

Among our other agents were Bill Miller, a former trumpet player; the Grace Sisters, a mother-and-daughter agency; and Marty Joyce in Columbus. We also worked for John Budniak, the orchestra leader whose wife, Helene, booked acts to work with the band, for DeArve Barton of MCA and for a few others. Vaudeville was far from dead in those days between the war and the arrival of television.

In 1947, Rennie Renfro offered me the job of running his kennel in Hollywood. Neal had left him to work for Rudd Weatherwax. He tried to win me over by telling me that I was the best and fastest trainer in the business. He also wanted me to go on a Hollywood-animal road show with Daisy's double and the pups. I wrote to him asking for a $70 weekly guarantee and ten percent of the gross. I wanted him to reduce the kennel size from 70 to 30 dogs. And, most important, I wanted his lawyer to draw up a contract, to be signed by me after my lawyer reviewed it. Another stipulation was a cash reserve fund to pay for any unexpected expenses. There was no reply. He did call me later about the road show, which he had contracted to organize. The first performance was booked by MCA and scheduled for Wilmington, Ohio. Taking my annual one-week leave to test out this adventure, I traveled to Wilmington with Smoky.

Because of mechanical troubles, the bus from California, carrying all the people and animals, was a day late. We greeted Rennie and his wife, Maddie, and her brother, Ray, who had driven a station wagon behind the bus. Maddie and Ray were a top trick-roping act in Ken Murray's Blackouts. Rennie brought Daisy, Daisy's double and the pups. The convoy also included a house trailer pulled by a pick-up truck. The trailer was divided into two sections. In the front were living quarters for the half-Indian, Okachobee Joe, and his driver/helper. In the back there was space for the beautiful chestnut horse, Gallant Bess, named for the movie in which he starred about a Japanese cavalry horse captured in New Guinea.

The bus was a miniature Noah's Ark. The front was fitted with seats for 10 passengers and the back served as quarters for the menagerie, including several eagles, the Pathe rooster, a trained mountain lion, a buzzard, a black bear and the Daisy pups. There was also a large covered cage filled with trained canaries riding with the passengers.

We carried the animal cages backstage. A golden eagle was terrified after the long ride in the darkened bus. It stood on its perch, swung its head around in a complete circle and tumbled off the perch. It climbed back up onto the perch and again fell off. We were sure it was having a nervous breakdown. Two of us picked up its cage, it flew at my fingers with its beak. Swinging the heavy cage out and away from my face a muscle pulled in my sacroiliac. The eagle recovered.

The first of three performances was scheduled for the next day. Although the show was a bit rough around the edges, it was a good show and played to an appreciative full house. It opened with Ray and Maddie's fast-moving roping act. Gallant Bess, the magnificently trained horse, followed. He was introduced as a movie star. "Bess" was actually a gelding. The use of male animals in female parts originated when producers realized that maternity leaves might slow down production. The theater was strictly a movie house and the stage was only four feet wide. There was no backstage area, so Bess had to come down the main aisle. The horse walked slowly through the theater, carefully stepping over kids' feet, and was led up the stairs by the ever-unruffled Okachobee Joe.

Bess did all his tricks flawlessly, responding to voice commands. "Take off my hat, Bess." He did. "Take my handkerchief from my back pocket, Bess." He did. Bess swung around the narrow stage as if it were an acre of pastureland. He rolled on the floor, played dead and pawed the answers to addition and subtraction problems. He finished the act with his impression of Frederick Remington's famous horse sculpture, "End of the Trail."

An unusual bird act was always a big hit. A little white-haired lady with a flock of yellow canaries performed in a darkened theater, illuminated by only a bright light on a table. The birds, flying freely about, returned, on signal, to the table where they pulled wagons, rode seesaws, did hand tricks and sang on command. When they finished, they flew back to their perches. Even when a bird flew out into the audience, it always returned. The secret was the blacked-out theater.

The Pathe rooster, who introduced the Pathe movie news, crowed on cue, never disappointing an audience. Rennie and Daisy and the pups were a strong finish for the show. Smoky was not performing this time around.

My back was so bad as a result of the eagle-lifting incident it was almost impossible to walk. There was a doctor across the street from the theater, but he was not a chiropractor. He said he had been practicing some manipulation techniques and offered to try to ease my pain. He did a terrific job, and I was able to help load the caravan for our next date, 300 miles away in West Virginia. We jostled and bounced in the bus for eight hours and barely had enough time to set up again for the four shows on this stop. Then we bumped along all night to Indiana for another three shows. My back was killing me. Next, we drove to Louisville, Kentucky.

We were all showing signs of fatigue from the lack of sleep and the endless performances.

The person who dreamed up this schedule must have had a desk job. Our next scheduled stop was Sandusky, Ohio, located in Northern Ohio. I went to Rennie and Ray and told them my job was waiting and I was going home. They were shocked. They offered me a small amount of expense money, but when I showed them my actual expenses, they gave me more. Rennie said he would call me when he wanted me to take over his part in the show.

My father-in-law drove Margie and my mother to the theater in Sandusky. I was in horrible pain all the way home. The next day, a famous Cleveland chiropractor nearly broke my back with his adjustments. If I tightened up, he'd say, "Okay, if you're going to fight me, let's quit right now." There was improvement as a result of his manhandling, but it was difficult to decide what had been worse, the pain or the treatment.

During my few days with the show, I had learned a bit more about the real Daisy. All the great trained dogs have little idiosyncrasies. Lassie (Pal) was a motorcycle chaser. Well, Rennie asked me to take Daisy to the station wagon. On my way back alone, Rennie saw me, he panicked. "My god!" he yelled. "You can't leave Daisy alone in a car. He eats everything made of leather. He'll eat all that upholstery."

Back at work the de-icing flights continued. On one flight, we took on seven inches of ice in 70 seconds and lost 70 miles per hour airspeed.

A short time later, Rennie called again. It was time for me to join the troupe. It was thanks, but no thanks. The crew was scheduled to do some research in Alaska, about as far away as I could imagine. I had no way of knowing where our next flights might take us.

Wanting to get another Yorkie, I made arrangements with Goldie to get a pet-type dog, not a show dog. These sell for a lot less but carry the genes of the better dogs. The dog she sent me resembled one of her finer studs. She never showed that dog, but he sired many champions. His offspring had good color and his pups never had under-shot or over-shot jaws.

Color and hair texture are important features in the Yorkshire Terrier. Goldie always bred to produce the darker steel blue and brilliant gold colors. To get this she said you had to have the silver blues in the breeding or the gunmetal blues eventually breed blacker and black begins to creep in to the golden fawn heads making them "sootie." Our pup weighed about

118

five pounds and was too large to be shown. The show standard allows this size, but the champions were traditionally under four pounds.

When Jack Lewis first saw the little guy, he laughed, "Hey, it's Mr. Terrific." The name stuck and we called him Terry for short. At seven months, he was a sweet puppy. Two weeks later, Smoky came into season, with a strong reproductive drive. I placed Terry in a pen surrounded by chicken wire 14 inches high. Herself jumped into the pen with the pup and had her way with him. My brother, Jim, came home and found the two little lovers together, wagging their tails happily. We removed Smoky from Terry's company, but she had accomplished what she set out to do. Just a week later, Jim put Terry out in the back yard, and the puppy disappeared. We searched everywhere. I put pictures of him on telephone poles and ran ads in the paper, offering a reward. Now I understood the feelings of the person who had lost Smoky in New Guinea. Terry was never found.

On June 27, 1947, Smoky began showing signs that she was nearing delivery of her pup. I wanted her to have the best care, so I took her in to our vet. Yorkies can be at risk during delivery and frequently need help. She delivered one small puppy with no trouble at all, and we were all relieved.

On June 28, 1947, at 9:27 a.m., Joanne Marie, the first of our nine children, was born. As fate would have it I had promised Fletcher Reynolds, the zoo director, that I would appear with Smoky for a very important affair. We were due there at 11:00 a.m. By 10:00 a.m. after Margie delivered I went to the vet, picked up Smoky and the two-day-old pup and reported at the zoo. Margie had been in labor all night. Hurrying through everything I made it back to the hospital by 1:00 p.m. Margie was feeling much better. But she never forgot the competition for this important time.

We were in the postwar baby boom, and fathers had to wait in long lines to see their babies through glassed-in nursery windows. In those days, we were not permitted to be with the mothers during delivery nor were we allowed to hold our new babies right away.

When Smoky's pup was four months old, we gave her to Margie's sister, Helen. Two months later, Helen called to tell us that the puppy was deathly ill after running loose in the yard. I rushed it to Dr. Wendt. He said it looked bad. Whatever the pup had eaten outdoors had been awfully rancid. The poor little fellow died. We just had bad luck with Smoky's puppies.

Smoky and I continued working weekend dates. Fourth of July, Halloween and Christmas always proved to be our best bookings. Joe Lorz, a Cleveland Heights' High teacher and a city recreation director, gave us lots of work through the years. We encountered some unusual hazards during those Fourth of July dates. In one instance at Clague Park several people were seriously injured when an aerial bomb toppled over and fired into the crowd.

Another time, in Cleveland Heights, I took my dogs as far away as possible before the shooting started, because Smoky had never gotten over her sensitivity to loud booms. This day, it had rained heavily and the fireworks were soaked. The fireworks' professionals lighted them and some of the rockets hopped, skipped and jumped to the other displays, setting them off. Others burst out sideways, shooting rockets and aerial bombs all over the place. The wet wicks caused some to delay firing until long after they should have, while others exploded prematurely. It was a good thing we were ducking behind the parked cars, because an aerial bomb flew right at us and exploded a short distance away.

American Magazine called to say they were sending Hans Knoph, a New York photographer, to take pictures of Smoky. She had been selected as one of the four most useful dogs in America, in a Gaines dog food contest. Gaines had been impressed with our entry and agreed that Smoky was a remarkable dog, but they said they were looking for working farm dogs. American Magazine made the selections, however, and Smoky was among the four dogs chosen. The magazine wrote, "Most dog owners work for their dogs, but these dogs work for their masters, and were selected as 'The Most Useful Dogs in America.' " It was a great honor for a little jungle dog.

One day, while trying on a new suit, I noticed the shop had some racks made from chrome-plated, one-inch pipes attached to four legs and fitted with rollers to hang up the suits and jackets. I thought that with some modifications, the design might lend itself to the construction of a new tightwire rig. The wooden one made by Mr. Lovejoy was getting rickety and its paint needed constant touch-ups.

One of the racks was purchased from the clothing store supplier of furnishings, and my father-in-law, George Roberts, worked on it for me. He produced a rig that was simple to break down and reassemble, so that it was portable and easily fit into a car. I had a collapsible ladder made, too. New steel cable was attached to new platforms at each end of the apparatus. Margie's dad also designed a grooved, wooden rack that kept the many pipes in place when I transported the rig.

We continued our stage work, although in 1948-49 we had no car. We had sold the Packard to get a down payment on a house. Edgar Wong, a chemical-research engineer, who lived nearby, shared his car with me. Because of its size and its 12 miles-per-gallon, the Packard was hard to sell. Eventually, we got $825 for it after I practically begged the guy to take it. Two years later, he tried to sell it or trade it in on a new car. The dealer asked if he had anything else to trade. He replied that he had a 1936 Ford in his yard that had been dead for two years. "Tow it in," the dealer said, "and I'll give you $250 for it." That beautiful Packard was taken to the junk yard and sold for scrap.

We really needed our own home. Margie's parents were wonderful, but we had been staying with them for too long and our family was growing. Joanne and Billy were our first two contributions to the baby boom. Susan soon followed.

My brother, Jim, owned a military-style Willys Jeep with a canvas roof, canvas side curtains, isinglass windows, loose doors and no heater. He installed a Sears Roebuck gas heater, which was a fine heater, but not for this drafty two-seater. The passenger's right foot got cooked, but the rest of his body was as stone cold as the driver's. Jim occasionally loaned me that Jeep even though it was his only car.

The act was scheduled to make several trips to Pennsylvania to appear in nightclubs in Oil City, Union City and a couple of other towns. It was the dead of winter and temperatures had hit bottom. Once, the emcee of the show asked to ride with me on the long trip. He showed up wearing only a tuxedo. He ignored my suggestion he find something a bit warmer, saying he never got cold. I was dressed in my suit, a topcoat, an extra pair of trousers and a war-surplus parka with a fur-lined hood. Smoky was tucked into the front of the parka with only her nose sticking out. I never saw anyone get colder faster than that poor emcee. Twenty minutes into the drive he had his collar up around his neck and was wearing my knit cap. It was 100 miles to our destination.

On one of those club dates, we arrived during a snowstorm. The temperature was below zero and two patrons showed up. In true show business tradition, the proprietor proclaimed that the show must go on, but not beyond the first performance. The cooks, waitresses, bus boys, hat check girl and the two customers enjoyed the show. The band never showed up. On this trip, we passed a lot of stalled cars and were happy to have the four-wheel-drive.

For years after the war, there were waiting lists for new cars. In 1949, we bought a nice 1937 Ford Tudor sedan for $200. We got the car just in time for the big Buffalo Allbreed Dog Show, where Smoky was to be one of the attractions. We were paid an extra $200 to come two days early to appear on several radio broadcasts as a promotion for the weekend show. Adam Eby and Associates handled the arrangements and did such a great job that I tried to persuade Eby to manage our act. He declined. Like so many other agents, he was not sure how to handle us, because we were out of the mainstream in show business.

It began to snow heavily in Buffalo, with the white stuff piling up 12 inches. I bought some tire chains and installed them, so we had no trouble getting to all our assignments. There were two other acts in the show. One was a retired police chief from New Jersey and his Golden Retriever. The dog had been used in police work and the two gave excellent obedience-training demonstrations. The other act was Willie Necker and his Dalmatians, a variety act featuring jumping dogs. Necker had been a high-ranking Coast Guard officer and had supervised the training of the dogs the Coast Guard used extensively on patrols.

We did three performances a day on Saturday and Sunday. Because of the advance publicity, the show drew more than 10,000 people, which was truly amazing, considering the weather.

We left Buffalo on Sunday night to get back to my regular job on Monday. The roads and visibility were so bad that following 50 feet behind a semi doing 50 m.p.h. seemed the most sensible thing to do. We were so close to him that, if he had plunged into Lake Erie, Smoky and I would have followed him right in. I said to Smoky beside me, "Lets give 'er a go mite!" (All long A's are long I's in Australian dialect.)

In the spring, on opening the trunk of the Ford, I discovered that the spare tire was firmly padlocked in place to prevent theft. We had no key. The tire clamp had to be sawed off. Margie says that the Lord always took good care of me. I shudder when I think of the number of times we braved the elements, confident because we had our spare tire in place.

Television had come to the Cleveland area in 1947. A guy in our photo lab paid $350 for a set with a 10-inch picture tube. As yet, no station was broadcasting anything but a test pattern, so people sat around for months watching the test pattern. Smoky and I were booked on the "Polka

Review," Ch. 5 WEWS one of the first programs telecast on Saturday nights.

In ten years of performing, Smoky relieved herself on stage only twice. A short walk before a show was standard routine. I regulated her food intake carefully, both in the amount and the kinds of food she consumed, as well as when she ate it. You can imagine my distress when, during our first live TV appearance, Smoky began doing the little turnaround that indicated she was looking for a dropping spot. She had been jumping hurdles and stopped cold after the third one. The band was playing, "Oh, Where Oh Where Has My Little Dog Gone," which was surprisingly appropriate. Kneeling down at the side of the stage, I called out, "What did we do in the foxhole. Smoky?" She came over to me, put her feet and head on my knee in a praying position and ad-libbed the dropping. The band played on, and the camera never caught the action. I walked her to the center of the stage and asked her what it had been like overseas. She sneezed out, "Rough!" which always elicited laughter and applause. We finished the show.

A couple of years later, when we played with a popular dance band at Vermilion, Ohio, the same thing happened. Only this time she relieved herself in plain sight before I could do anything about it. A trumpet player rose from his chair, picked up some tissues from a box at his side and high-stepped out onto the stage. The drummer picked up his beat. "Ta dum, ta dum, de boop de boop, ta dum." The trumpeter bent over, scooped up the deposit and marched back to his chair to "ta dum, ta dum, de boop de boop, ta dum." The audience howled. Those two episodes will remain with me forever.

In late 1949, the flight surgeon discovered that I had a broken eardrum, and was immediately grounded. The de-icing program was in its last year. We were aviation pioneers, but we didn't know it at the time. For the almost 50 years since then all commercial and military aircraft have used the equipment we tested.

As Smoky and I continued our early television work, Margie presented me with a fourth child, Marcia. WXEL, Channel 9 (now WJW, Channel 8), the third station in Cleveland broadcasting, was organized for $400,000 by the owner of Empire Coil and Spring. The transmitter and studios were located on a high hill in Parma, Ohio. We came in for an audition and found the studio in chaos. The first live show had been a disaster and most of the talent and the work force had just been fired.

A children's show, "Castles in the Air," had a 5 p.m. time slot. It was hosted by a charming woman, Pat Ryan. Pat was called the Cloud Lady and dressed in a long, flowing, gray cloak. Pat and the station manager liked our audition and promised me they would call. They did call and invited us to appear on "Castles" once a week, on Fridays.

Shows were generally booked for 13 or 26 weeks. We were asked to do 13. Pat said we would make a brief appearance and Smoky would do just one trick each time. Pat was always in costume, so I decided to surprise her with a costumed character of my own. We ripped an old suit coat and sewed patches on my trousers. Two burlap bags tied with hemp covered my shoes. I borrowed a black derby from a friend and wore it on top of a bright yellow wig. A big, glued-on nose was my finishing touch.

For years harmonica playing had been a hobby. Now, for the act, I perfected my musical talent and worked out a tune called "Mr. Pokie and His Dog, Smoky," adding the lyrics to entertain my children. This song has been sung for three generations of our family.

Oh, Mr. Pokie, where are you?
Mr. Pokie, where are you?
Why, there he is, right over there
With his big nose and yellow hair.
Smoky is his little dog.
They know how to jump and jog.
They are quite a jolly pair,
With their big noses and yellow hair.

When we showed up at the studio, Pat did not see my costume. She was on stage working out the camera angles and positions with the floor director and the producer. When we did make our entrance to the tune of "Mr. Pokie," she laughed to see Smoky tugging on a leash with an old tramp at the end of it. When she asked, "Who are you?"

I replied in a high-pitched voice, "Mr. Pokie and my dog, Smoky."

I was not trying a stage voice, but was so nervous that my voice turned high and squeaky. The act was a hit and, from then on, I had to keep the voice in because it was part of the overall impression. After we did our trick, the Cloud Lady announced that Mr. Pokie and his dog, Smoky, were going back to the Dog Star and that we would be back the following Friday.

Every Friday for the next 42 weeks, we came from the Dog Star to do a trick for children who were lucky enough to have a TV set. The show generated a club called the Little Ajax Club and lots of kids signed up, giving the station some idea of our following.

With the $15 we earned for each performance, we purchased a 10-inch Crosley TV for our children.

Smoky is mentioned in "The Guinness Book of Almost Everything You Didn't Need to Know About Dogs," by Valerie Porter. In the war hero subheading, she writes about Smoky's pulling the wires through the pipe. I wish she had written about our doing 42 television shows without repeating a trick. I asked her about that later and she replied, "I was asked to produce a list of dogs and could only include the briefest reference to each one."

On Fridays, I took Smoky, in her traveling bag, to work at the lab. Using one hour leave time to get off early, we rushed to make it to the station before five o'clock. I was in costume and on camera by 5:20. It was really a fun show.

Because we were so popular on "Castles," we were asked to do quite a few other shows. We played for the kids at Rainbow Hospital for Children and at the Society for Crippled Children. During that period, we also had regular club dates and were booked at a number of society events, particularly for the Junior League.

Gene Carroll hired us to appear at the Palace Theater. Gene had been the emcee of a professional variety stage show before he began his popular TV amateur hour. He became famous for the 1930s radio shows, "The Gene and Glenn Show" with "Jake and Lena." When they appeared in public, their audience formed lines that stretched around the block. On the radio, Gene played himself and the voices of Jake and Lena. Glenn played the straight man and the piano. They both sang well. Gene did his Lena on the national "Fibber McGee and Molly" broadcasts.

Smoky and I did an occasional county fair and even did a bit for an early telethon, telecast from a downtown theater stage. About this time, Robby, our fifth child was born. Smoky was still going strong, but I decided to train another dog, Patch, to give her a break now and then. Patch, a large Dalmatian, had been advertised for sale for $10. He was an impressive physical specimen with a large black patch over his right eye. For Dalmatians the desired markings are small black spots, and he was a bit oversize, so Patch was not a show dog.

The day we brought the dog home, he raced outside and grabbed the mailman by the ankle. The poor guy wasn't hurt, but Patch scared the bejeebers out of him. This problem needed to be solved, pronto. I met the mailman on the street the next day and asked if he would cooperate in a plan. Opening the garage door just a few inches he was asked to put some dog kibbles under the door for Patch, who gulped them down eagerly. In just three days, Patch was waiting for the mailman with his tail wagging. Before long, he was meeting the mailman outside. I called Patch's previous owner who told me they had really enjoyed the dog, but couldn't deal with the mailman problem. The dog had been frightened by a paper boy who swung his bag at him and had been suspicious ever after of anyone carrying a large bag.

Patch learned to walk on his hind legs, carrying a big stick with a parakeet at each end. He learned to roll over on command and mastered a few other tricks but, although he would do these tricks perfectly during practice, he did whatever he wanted on stage.

I'd say, "Sit up," and he'd lie down. I'd say, "Lie down," and he'd walk around on his hind legs. For the audience, I'd pretend that he was making a fool of me, and they'd roar. (Actually, he was making a fool of me.) Every now and again, I would ask him to do something and he'd do it right but, for the audience, that was not as much fun.

For several years, Patch was used to stretch our show. Smaller groups usually didn't pay us much, but they always wanted a long show. With Smoky alone, the act often ran 30 to 40 minutes. Besides the dead dog trick, she did wire walking, jumped the hurdles and worked with the ladder, the sliding board and the drum. Sometimes we brought up volunteers from the audience to show off our Hollywood tricks. Smoky would be ordered to stay with the volunteer as he walked around the stage. She was quite an actress. She looked up into the person's face and barked for him or she would sit up and give him a kiss or sing for him. With demonstrations of both hand and voice signals, we rounded out the long program. In the big time, with name acts our act had to be fast-moving and short, seven minutes at the most.

After a while, I wasn't using Patch much any more, so we passed him along to a mother and daughter who said they would like to have him. Patch had a fear of thunder. The big dog could sense a storm two days in advance. His tongue and mouth turned a deep red and he became terribly nervous. After the two ladies had owned him for two years, his fear became worse. A veterinarian told them that such a big dog might be unintentionally dangerous in his panic during thunderstorms. He was put to sleep. Today tranquilizers are available to deal with such problems.

One of our vaudeville dates took us to an outdoor theater in Newcomerstown, Ohio, where the stage was set in front of a huge screen. The wind was wild on two nights of the week-long stand, and Smoky's wire walking was difficult. The only time she ever fell was during that windstorm. I caught her, unharmed, put her back up on the wire and she gamely walked across with her tail wagging.

The Columbus, Ohio, theatrical agent, Marty Joyce, booked us often. One appearance was so successful that the audience applauded our every move. We received a standing ovation with three curtain calls. I had them, as Marty told me later, "in the palm of my hand."

Some audiences are like that. They appreciate the small-time acts as much as they appreciate the big stars. Many of the smaller acts could have made it to the big-time. Often personal choices kept them from it. The players preferred a simpler life. There is tremendous pressure to succeed in the star arena. The customers pay big money to see you and they demand to be amused and entertained, but the shows are always well-produced and the audience is satisfied. Some acts just don't like the travel or the pace and prefer to stay happy where they are.

Marty Joyce recognized the fact that Smoky was aging and encouraged me to become an emcee on my own, but I was not interested. We worked with some name band leaders like Clint Noble, Blue Baron and Frankie Yankovic. We occasionally played with Emmett Kelly. Harvey Firestone, Jr. invited us to participate in a week-long show for his employees in Akron, Ohio. The Firestone Rubber Company had thousands of employees, so we did two shows a day to entertain them all including their families at Christmas parties held in a large movie theater. Mr. Firestone attended almost every party.

My favorite booker was John Budniak, the band leader. His shows were always supercharged and John loved to have his band play for every act. He smiled broadly and enjoyed the show more than anyone else. His music was a wonderful background for all of us because he put his heart into his piano playing. When the show was over, the audience was always "in the palm of your hand."

CHAPTER 12

THE MYSTERY IS SOLVED

On Columbus Day, 1953, I visited Ted Vorpe, the editor of the Plain Dealer Sunday Magazine and director of photography for the paper. Ted had run some of my work in this pictorial supplement. He had used color layouts from NACA and, more recently, a photo essay called "Suicide Camera." This layout included scenes shot by a K24 aerial camera, three shots per second, as it dropped from the 125-foot High Level Bridge over the Cuyahoga River. I had attached a Bungee shock cord to keep my camera alive.

Ted was surprised to see me downtown on a holiday, but he asked me a question that surprised me even more. "Bill, would you consider coming to work for the Plain Dealer?" he queried.

Somewhat taken aback, I replied, "Gee, Ted, I don't know. I wouldn't like covering hard news and I would hate working the night shift." (The Plain Dealer is a morning paper.)

"Well," he said, "One of our photographers as been diagnosed as having multiple sclerosis and we are not sure what his status will be. We need someone who knows color and who can step right in. Your assignments will be in advertising, the Sunday magazine and the Sunday features department. There will be no hard news coverage. It's a day job, 9:00 to 5:00, and the pay will be $105 a week. And, a pay raise is being negotiated with the Newspaper Guild right now."

The salary being offered was a third more than what I was making at NACA. I asked Ted if he would give me a week to talk it over with my wife. He said, "Sure, call me when you make up your mind." I conferred with my boss at NACA who checked out my prospects and told me that it would take six years for me to reach that pay scale.

Our sixth child, Donna, had arrived and I really needed the additional money. I had no choice but to make the switch. On November 4, 1953, my career as a Cleveland Plain Dealer photographer began. Later, I would become a writer/photographer. My association with the paper continued for 31 years. Early in 1954, I decided to retire from show business, even though Smoky was still in fine shape. The Sunday pictorial carried an article and photo telling of Smoky's retirement after a 10-year career.

Not long after that, I received a call from Maggie Chute, a public relations promoter, who suggested that we audition for a new Sunday morning TV show WNBK Ch. 3. It would last two hours and would include cartoons and live presentations. Sunday morning TV had notoriously low ratings and most channels just showed cartoons. I explained to Maggie that we had retired. But she thought I could do a 15- minute segment, featuring Smoky for just one trick, training a green dog and then interviewing a guest from the dog world. We auditioned. Smoky came out of retirement to work with me on our program, "How To Train Your Dog, with Bill Wynne and Smoky." Also on the show were "Pat Paterson's Outdoors," a professional golf teacher, and Glenn Rowell (from the Gene and Glenn radio show), doing a song and piano segment. We were scheduled to run 13 weeks.

I opened alone and then had Smoky do a trick while we demonstrated how that trick could be taught. After that, I would bring on my guest, an expert in obedience training, or a dog writer, or someone prominent in dog showing and breeding. We featured lots of dogs and the show went from near zero in the ratings to a very high audience share.

We were getting letters from all over our area and from as far away as Canada. We had visitors. When people came to see her who hadn't come before and seated in the living room Smoky's shimmering silken gold and silver coat flowed lively as she pranced in to meet them. OOOHHS and AAAAHS greeted the bit of a dog as they reached down to touch her and she placed her tiny head into their outstretched hands. They were never disappointed for the little lady greeted each and everyone in her own audience style. It was a personal meeting they would never forget. Smoky knew she was something special, without being pompous. Barbara Wood Smith of the American Red Cross put it so grandly many years before, "a lady artiste without temperament."

One morning the station manager caught me by surprise. He introduced his sister, who ran a dog-training school in Canton, Ohio, and who had brought six other people and their dogs with her. Her brother had asked them to appear on my show. I had already booked a local dog class for that morning, but I didn't want to disappoint anyone, so I interviewed them all. People and dogs were flying on and off the set, in what must have been the busiest 15 minutes on television. Counting Smoky, 13 dogs were on the air that day.

It was strictly an ad-lib show. Before the show, I would talk to the floor manager about the upcoming sequence of events, and he would place the cameras in the best positions to cover the action. One of the producers suggested that Smoky and I do the segment alone. We tried this a couple of times, but I preferred the variety of guests. On one occasion famous big band leader Sammy Kaye delivered his beautiful 15 year old daughter to appear on our show with their family dog.

Sometimes I closed the show with a training demonstration, using a miniature platinum poodle loaned to me for the show. Caesar was a fine dog, but was somewhat overtrained in obedience. When I issued some of the obedience commands, he balked and became overly tense. When I taught him new tricks, he happily complied and seemed to enjoy it. Later, I used a previously untrained Cairn Terrier to close the show.

On one of our best shows, I asked my two-year-old daughter, Donna, to play with Smoky. I wanted to show my audience that when selecting a dog, the size of the dog should depend on the size of the child. Very small children should have big dogs for pets.

Donna reached out to grab Smoky's head and pulled on her mustache and sideburn and hairs and yanked her ear. This treatment will hurt a tiny dog and may cause it to snap at the child. A large dog would probably ignore the roughness. My daughter had illustrated my point. As the camera zoomed in for the closing shot. Donna leaned her little blonde head against my shoulder and Smoky rested her head on my other shoulder. Margie said it was a smash closing.

After 30 weeks, our show was cancelled when a new network took over the station and got rid of all the live shows. (This same network brought live local shows back later when it hired Mike Douglas. His program was very popular and widely syndicated.)

Smoky retired again, this time permanently.

From 1954 on, Smoky spent most of her time in her own little area of our house, away from the romping kids and the noisy bustle of a large household. In 1955, she developed a badly infected uterus. Dr. Wally Wendt saved our little four-pounder by performing a hysterectomy. Even a heart condition couldn't keep her down, and she remained spry and happy for the rest other life. Because of her heart, though, I carried her up and down stairs.

On February 21, 1957, I came home from work and found my little pal lying on her side, asleep in death. "Oh, no," I sighed in disbelief. I do not cry easily, but this time 1 could not hold back the tears. When I told Margie, she felt as bad for me as she did for Smoky.

We were going to be moving soon, so I didn't want to bury Smoky in our yard. I wanted her resting place to be a permanent one, a place we could visit and still keep secret.

Margie suggested "Our Tree" located deep in the woods of the Metro Park System. The Cleveland Metropark, known as The Emerald Necklace, is a gorgeous 50 miles of forests, rivers, cliffs and valleys surrounding the city. It would be an excellent place to lay my friend to rest.

The next day, Washington's Birthday 1957, the family, bundled against February's cold, drove to the Metro Park on Cleveland's west side. We were a somber group, marching slowly, single-file down Riverside Drive to our destination. I carried a shovel, a pick and, under my arm, a shoe box. We were on a burial detail.

The shoe box contained the remains of my tiny companion in war and peace. Nothing and no one interrupted our journey on that bleak day. We snaked down an incline and crossed a gorge to a path leading north. We walked through the black, leafless trees tinged with wet green moss until we came to a gray birch. Scanning the area from east to west, I spotted the bridle path I was looking for and led the way. Bumpy frozen hoofprints made the walking difficult. The children were stumbling and slipping. "It's just ahead," I assured them, hoping they would not lose heart.

At last we found "Our Tree." On its trunk was a large carved heart, weathered by time, but still a beautiful sight. Inside the heart were the initials B.W. above M.R. Underneath the letters, I had carved '40. Many years had passed since Margie and I had been here. We had carved the heart on our first bike hike together. That was in June 1940, and the tree was only eight inches in diameter.

About 13 feet from the tree, I located an open space near some sapling pines. I put the box down and began to dig. Margie and the children gathered silently around, and only the sounds of the shovel scraping the ground and the wind whispering through the barren trees broke that silence. Eventually, the grave was large enough to accommodate the shoe box. Gently, I set my beloved Smoky down into the little grave and as I started to cover the box with dirt, our seven-year-old, Susan, cried out, "Daddy, Daddy, how is Smoky going to breathe?"

I was caught unprepared. I hadn't wanted to talk about this now, but her bright blue eyes, brimming with tears, begged for an answer. "Smoky doesn't need to breathe any more," I whispered, "she is in dog heaven." I tried not to let my voice break, because Dads should be strong. I would not let them see my tears. I knelt down again, patting the little mound and gathering nearby stones for a grave marker, stalling for time to compose myself. After another moment of silence, our small band began the sad journey back to the car.

The Plain Dealer printed an obituary, written by Josephine Robertson, telling the story of the famous little dog of World War II. The day the item appeared in the paper, Margie got a call from a nurse at Crile Veterans Hospital.

"Mrs. Wynne," the caller said, "I read that your husband's little war mascot died. I don't know if this means anything, but I lost a female Yorkshire Terrier in Dobodura, New Guinea, early in 1944." She continued, "My fiance, now my husband, bought the puppy for me in 1943 from a veterinarian in Brisbane. She was a holiday gift, so I named her Christmas. The vet said the pup was too expensive for the average Aussie and sold her to us for 25 pounds Australian, about $80 American. That was a lot of money to the Australians because the American dollar had better purchasing power then."

Grace Guderian was a lieutenant assigned to a field hospital and was engaged to a Captain Heidenreich, assigned to the field artillery. They parted, going with their assigned units. Lt. Guderian took Christmas to New Guinea where the little dog was lost. Later, with special permission from General MacArthur, the couple was married in Manila. The wedding was covered by Yank Magazine, and we received a copy of that issue as a part of Smoky's prize. The cover photo showed a young couple coming down the church steps under an arch of crossed swords. She was from upstate New York but, after the war, they settled in his hometown, Cleveland. He worked for a brewery and she became the head of Crile's psychiatric ward until she retired.

I must assume that Christmas and Smoky were one and the same. So few Yorkies were bred worldwide during the war. England, the country of the breed's origination, had as few as 22 puppies registered in one war year. In 1945, only 65 puppies were registered in the U.S. I couldn't locate any Australian registrations for 1943 because the records were lost. The vet told Mrs. Heidenreich that he had registered the litter. She received papers, but didn't register her ownership. Also, the vet had told them how valuable the dog was, indicating that she was show quality.

Goldie Stone had testified to Smoky's quality when she told me she could sell a typy dog like mine for $250. When I got the dog, she was young and had her second teeth. I also remembered the time she reacted with such excitement to the word, Christmas. I had dismissed her response as a coincidence. She was about 14 when she died and there simply could not have been another female Yorkshire Terrier of her age and class lost in the New Guinea jungle.

But, how did she get to Nadzab? This is my scenario: Dobodora was located southeast of Nadzab and both were advance bases in territories our troops had taken from the Japanese. An extremely popular entertainer like Bob Hope, attracted flight personnel from all the bases in the area. Mrs. Heidenreich took her dog to the show and let it run loose. Christmas disappeared and, although she had everyone look for it, the dog was not found.

I assume that someone eventually found her wandering around and took her back with him to Nadzab, where the little tyke wandered off again and stumbled into the foxhole where Ed Downey found her.

This scenario relies heavily on coincidence, but it still seems the most plausible explanation of her appearance in my life.

I don't know why I became the guardian, tutor and companion of this spirited fluff of hair who shared our lives and fortunes—never misfortunes. My Yorkie Doodle Dandy, who could make Americans at war forget their troubles simply by watching her chase giant butterflies along the squadron roads. Her very presence unfailingly turned serious faces into smiles. Smoky's tiny brain permitted her to grasp things so quickly. Her lightening responses delighted audiences halfway around the world.

Do you suppose this little friend came into my care for my own well-being by the mystical—divine providence? There seems to have been very special reasons. My custodianship of Smoky helped me to deal with the pressure and loneliness of war. Loneliness, a carry over from my youth, offset when great dogs became the most important part of my life. Now, added to this she was such a great morale builder to others. One wonders, could this have been an angel in a foxhole—a buddy sent to teach me how to share her comical antics in a bigger task? That task being, the sharing her with others in a time when joy was scarce? Sometimes under stress it only takes a delightful moment of diversion from the path heading for mental disaster.

Whatever the reason, there was one more gift. It is more than evident Smoky taught me more than I ever taught her. Perhaps the most I learned was forcing myself to go on stage in front of audiences. She made it easier. Smoky was the star. They couldn't keep their eyes off of her. This way I gained confidence in myself, one of human beings' most difficult attributes to achieve.

Cleveland is 10,000 miles from the Nadzab, New Guinea jungle where Smoky was found. Doggone, if you think this tale isn't a little bizarre, consider this—when I visited the Heidenreich's, they lived within a few blocks of our house.

EPILOGUE

Sometimes people ask me how Margie and Smoky got along. I find that somewhat difficult to answer. Margie suggests that the book's dedication should read, "To my darling wife, Margie, who contributed absolutely nothing to encourage the writing of this book."

Margie and I were quiet kids. She was 17 and I was 18 when we met. Our ideals and plans for the future were simple, and we probably were mature beyond our years. In intellect and personality, we were well-suited to each other, although we were very different types. She was, by nature, a scholarly person and was raised by loving parents in a quiet home. I was a fatherless boy from a big supportive family, who grew up running in the streets, playing rough games and studying nature in the great outdoors. And of course I had a couple of great dog companions.

We had compatible goals, enjoyed the same music and followed the same religion. Although we didn't know each other at the time, we even attended the same grammar school. We dreamed of an amiable, serene, predictable future. The Great Depression was over and people were beginning to go back to work. We thought we might open a flower shop someday and, maybe, buy our own house. Our parents always rented, as did many of our neighbors.

Any plans for marriage were put on the back burner for a number of reasons. First, we wanted to work and save money for the future. Second, the threat of world war was ever present as, week after week, we read of Hitler swallowing his European neighbors. Margie went to work as a stenographer for the Cleveland Ordnance District and I began sweating in the steel mill, earning three times what my mother made during the '30s. We weren't sure where we were heading, especially after I was drafted in 1943. We corresponded almost daily and, on my furlough, we became engaged. Then I was shipped overseas, where an innocent little dog burst into my life and changed things forever. When Smoky and I came back, we were swept into a very public life style, so different from anything we had ever imagined.

Margie was caught unprepared. She was annoyed by the fanfare, and our lives were even more disrupted when we moved to Hollywood. She hated everything about Hollywood. Because we were flat broke and had little hope for a steady job and income there, she returned to Cleveland.

The intensity of her distress alarmed me. I decided not to pursue a career offered perhaps by producer, Owen Krump at Warner Brothers. I'm sure we would have been successful eventually, but I just couldn't picture Margie ever being happy in California. There are many paths available during one's lifetime. The one I chose was the only one for me. There was no way I was going to risk losing Margie.

But through the years, there was a trace of bitterness in my wife's heart. Did Margie hate Smoky? Not at all. She resented the changes that Smoky's presence dictated. The adulation given to a little dog displeased her. Margie saw the dog receiving more attention than was given to our own children. Several other things happened through the years. First, Margie never considered our Hollywood trip a honeymoon. That resentful memory was relieved with two recent trips to Ireland. The day before our first child Joanne was born Margie was upstaged by Smoky when she presented a pup by surprise and I had to dash off from the hospital shortly after Joanne's delivery with Smoky and two day old pup for a promised short appearance at the Cleveland Zoo. Halloweens were a nightmare for her with streams of children coming to trick or treat for four endless hours while she tried to take care of our little ones at dinner and bedtime. Of course, Smoky and I were doing Halloween parties at schools on those evenings. Then there were the two weeks of nightly children's Christmas parties all over town. These events continued for 10 years. She often told people that the "other woman was a real dog."

Did Smoky like Margie? "Not particularly," Margie says. Smoky was a one-man dog. In truth, she usually greeted my wife with less enthusiasm than she displayed for outsiders. Maybe she knew instinctively that Margie was her competition.

Does Margie like dogs? You bet she does, and she liked Smoky as a dog, but not as a star dog. When most of our children (we welcomed nine in all) went their separate ways, Margie took in a series of older dogs that others could no longer care for. Two of them were Yorkies. Later she brought home a German Wire-haired Pointer and, finally, a 10-year-old Miniature Poodle who lived with us for nine years. She was the proprietor of the old dogs' home.

For the first two years of our marriage, Margie and I lived with her parents in a small, two-bedroom apartment. Smoky, Toby and Lucky lived with my mother, brother and sister in a house 10 doors down from us. After our second child was born, we bought our first house and Smoky came to live with us.

136

By the time we bought our second house, our growing brood was endlessly pursuing, petting and pestering the tiny dog. She never evidenced any impatience with them if they handled her carefully, but she would snap in self-defense if the going got rough.

After so many years of living with our boisterous family. Smoky needed a quiet place of her own. I settled her into a newly constructed room taking up a quarter of the basement. If a window was covered it served as a dark room. When I worked there, she shared that time and space with me. When I was working elsewhere, the spacious room served as a quiet retreat for her. For several years we continued performing together, but only occasionally. After we retired Smoky, she enjoyed her tranquil life at home, happy even when cataracts dimmed her sight and her heart condition limited her activities.

Smoky and I shared certain personality traits. I never knew when she would balk at the training, either from stubbornness or boredom. I have a stubborn streak and react the same way at times. Some wonder if we instinctively choose pets to match our moods, or if we take on each other's characteristics over time. I believe that the latter is true.

Most people do not have the opportunity to share their pets with the world. Most do not have the joy of watching their pets bring so much pleasure to those who need a cheery moment in their lives. Millions saw Smoky on stage and on television. Her fan mail came from everywhere.

She was recognized as a great dog and a number of authors have recorded her accomplishments. In some of these books, my name is not mentioned.

Looking back, I no longer wonder that Ed Downey's jeep stalled at the very spot in the jungle where this little dog was stranded in a foxhole. Perhaps she was an angel in a foxhole. For what so ever the reason fate brought us together there is no doubt in my mind that Smoky and I were meant to be.

ADDENDUM

TRAINING THE SMALL DOG

Training any dog requires three important qualities on the part of the master, PATIENCE, PATIENCE, PATIENCE. Because the word, master, sounds so domineering, I prefer the word coach. Actually, you are a team working together so think of yourselves as teammates. But, one of the team must show the way. Although you see dogs dragging around their hapless owners, the dog should not be the one in charge. Before I begin to discuss training, I must tell you how to recognize trainability potential in a dog.

In Smoky's case, I was very lucky. She had been well handled before I got her. She would have passed any screening test. Her early care by Grace Heidenreich formed this little dog's character, her loving nature and her trainability. Among Hollywood animal trainers there is a system for picking the best dogs. It may help you to test your dog. Many movie dogs come from dog pounds and are unfamiliar with the trainers. You can find great dogs at the pound if you know what to look for. Most of these dogs were picked up as strays or were turned in, reluctantly, by owners who hoped their pets might be adopted.

Movie dogs are at least one year old, because the trainer does not have the time to wait for a puppy to mature. Professional athletes are not chosen when they are five years old. An old dog does not have the life expectancy to warrant the training and larger dogs do not usually live as long as the smaller breeds. Dogs with short noses, such as the English Bulldog and the Pekinese, may develop breathing problems earlier.

I am often surprised by the quality of some of the dogs at the pound. Not only is their breeding good, but their dog-to-human attitudes are healthy.

Here is the test that Hollywood trainers use. (NOTE: A NOVICE TRAINER SHOULD NOT TRY TO TEST A STRANGE DOG'S AGGRESSIVENESS.) An experienced trainer can sense how far he can go with a strange dog, the novice may not have developed this instinct. You probably know your own pet well enough to test its aggressiveness.

1. Is the dog curious?

At the pound, did he stand when you approached his cage? That is a good sign, but even a good dog can be too discouraged by his surroundings to respond instantly to your presence. Hide a squeaky toy behind your back and squeak it several times. Does the dog cock his head? Does he move his head back and forth at the sound? If so, he has curiosity, an important quality in training. If he is listless, this is not the dog you are looking for.

2. Is he aggressive?

If the dog seems friendly, have an attendant take your candidate out of the cage. Is the dog's tail wagging? Does he seem happy to see you and the others who may be there? Does he seem energetic and healthy? Using a glove or a piece of cloth, invite the dog to play tug-of-war with you. If you feel comfortable with the dog, encourage him to wrestle GENTLY with your sleeve-covered arm. If he enjoys this wrestling play, he shows significant aggressiveness, another characteristic required in training. If he won't wrestle, he has failed the test.

3. Is he controllable?

Assuming he has responded to the playful challenge, after 10 seconds call out, NO, to tell the dog to stop. If he stops, he is controllable and has passed the test. If he continues to wrestle, cuff him lightly under the chin, calling out, NO. If he stops then, he is still a good candidate. If he does not want to stop, even after the cuff, he has failed the test.

For dogs passing this three-step test, the sky is the limit, providing the trainer is an excellent one. These are the dogs you see starring in the movies.

TRAINING "PRINCE"

Perhaps you have not had the opportunity to choose a dog of the right age and trainability. Your dog is six months to a year old. We'll call him "Prince." Let's begin.

In your training vocabulary, the most important word is NO. If the puppy is chewing on your fingers as you hold him, say, NO, and cuff him gently under the chin.

NASA researcher Jerry Pesman was always telling us about bears in the wild. Jerry said the mother bear will cuff her cub when it is doing something wrong. If the cub is playing too rough with one of its siblings, the mother will saunter over and give it a cuff. If the cub does not respond, the next cuff will send it tumbling end over end. You will not need to be this tough in training your dog, but you must make sure the dog gets your message.

Use NO in other situations. If Prince is about to relieve himself in the house, say, NO. Quickly pick him up and take him to a place where he is allowed to relieve himself and, when he does, praise him with, GOOD DOG. GOOD PRINCE.

The leash and collar become the instruments of communication with your dog. Start with a leather collar that is tight enough to stay on the dog if he backs away from you, but the collar should be comfortable. In this early training, the dog is learning to respond to its name, learning right from wrong and learning when and where certain behavior is acceptable. At first, the leash may simply be a piece of a cord strong enough to manage the dog's weight and strength or, if you choose, a leather leash with a snap-on clasp for a collar ring.

Call your dog, COME, PRINCE, gently but firmly pulling the leash to bring him toward you. Squat down to meet the dog on his level. As he comes, praise him, GOOD DOG. You are friends and you want to maintain that friendship during training. Eventually, you will extend the leash to 20 feet, using cord or rope. You want to be able to control your dog from a distance.

TEACHING TO HEEL

It is important at this point to emphasize <u>short</u> training periods of 5 to 7 minutes with play in between. Training must be interesting and fun. <u>Remember</u> five 5-minute periods of training is better than a half hour straight.

After Prince knows the meaning of NO, you can teach him to COME, HEEL, SIT and STAY on command. Start walking with the dog on the leash. For a small dog, the leash will work well, but a choke collar is used on a larger dog. This is a chain with a steel loop on each end. The chain is made into a lasso and placed on the dog so that the dangling end is close to your left side.

At first he may wander off to the end of the leash or walk between your legs. In either case, call him back to your side with NO. Tug the leash sharply to get his attention and keep him on your left with his chest aligned to your left knee. DO NOT KEEP A TIGHT LEASH TO HOLD THE DOG AT THIS POSITION. Rather, use a series of short tugs to remind the dog where he is supposed to be. Using this jerk and release technique is less uncomfortable for the dog and he will respond more enthusiastically to your commands, recognizing that his obedience released the pressure on his neck.

If he moves forward too far, say, HEEL or PRINCE, HEEL, giving a jerk on the collar. If he drags, jerk him forward, repeating the HEEL command to keep him at your knee. Keep the leash slack, dangling it about four inches from the collar ring. A larger dog may lean against your knee. If that happens, nudge him away as you walk, jerking the chain collar. Tiny dogs learn very early to keep away from your feet, realizing that they may fall underfoot and get hurt.

Smoky was very bright. I had to work to stay ahead of her during her training. When I was teaching her to heel, she knew immediately when the leash was off, and she wouldn't obey. I fastened two strong light cords to her collar, in addition to the leash. When I removed the leash and she started to do her own thing, I yanked on one of the other cords and commanded, SMOKY, HEEL! That got her attention. Then I unfastened the cord and ordered her to HEEL. Thinking she was loose, she started forward again and I jerked the other cord. After that, she was never quite sure if she was connected or not and she heeled perfectly. If your dog resists you, try to figure a way to outsmart him.

Animals are able to size people up instinctively. Riding stables try to use good old, dependable horses that are safe for their clients. Savvy horses can tell if the rider is inexperienced and may react in a way dangerous to the rider. In a similar way, some dogs may be too spirited for the average family.

During obedience training, DO NOT GIVE YOUR DOG TREATS TO MOTIVATE HIM. The fastest way to train Prince may be with food as a reward. You see this practice at work at the circus or other animal shows. It may make the animal eager to perform, but when used by an inexperienced trainer, it may make the animal too eager. I do not recommend this for regular training. If you run out of the treats, the animal will not perform.

SMOKY NEVER RECEIVED TREATS FOR ANY OF HER TRICKS.

For those of you who are novices, don't try to teach any tricks before you have mastered the control of your dog through obedience training. First he must understand, HEEL, SIT, SIT-STAY, DOWN-STAY and COME. In the long run, your dog will see your pleasure when he obeys and he will obey to make you happy. No treats will be needed. Continue to show your pleasure with his work and you will become a team. With really hard work, you will become a precision team.

There are books on obedience training for dogs to be used in competition and these rules change ever so slightly through time. I have not consulted these books for my training techniques, preferring to write from my own experience. You can borrow these books from the library or purchase them at book stores.

The basic obedience rules contain the fundamental calls and orders for your dog to obey if it is going to fit into your household and behave like a lady or gentleman in your home and in public. A civilized dog must come when called, as well as sit, lie down and stay when told to.

STAND STAY

For dog shows, a dog must learn to STAND STAY. Judges at these shows walk around the dog and feel its form for defects which may be hidden under its hair.

Dogs in the ring are asked to be trained so that the judge may move quickly from one dog to another. There may be a thousand dogs in a show. A show dog must not sit down when a judge presses down on its hips. One way to teach your dog not to sit in this situation is to place your finger under his belly when he is standing and press down on his back. When he starts to sit, push your finger up into his belly and command, STAND STAY. He will stand up. Repeat the exercise. When he remains standing when you press down on his back, praise him with, GOOD PRINCE. GOOD DOG.

STAND STAY is also a must command for halting a moving dog. If he has learned this command, he will stop cold immediately. In the Philippines, Smoky was saved by her immediate response to STAND STAY. She froze in her tracks, inches away from the rumbling wheels of a truck. I was 50 feet from her, but she obeyed. The dog must learn to freeze when you command, STAND STAY. Then, call him to you. PRINCE, COME will not stop a running dog immediately. Instead, the dog will make a wide, forward moving curve in returning to you..

To teach STAND STAY, tie the leash to a tree or have someone else hold the leash. Call the dog to you. When he is near the end of the leash, command, STAND STAY. If he doesn't stop, he will get a jar when he reaches the end of the leash. When he learns to stop on command, praise him. If you are also training with hand signals, extend your arm and hand, palm up, to hold him off. Then approach him, making him hold his ground, as you walk around behind him and stand at his right side. Then have him SIT. You may practice this command either by walking toward your dog or calling him to you. Release him from the STAND STAY with ALL RIGHT or OK.

Your dog must learn to respond to verbal commands because he will not always be facing you. Suppose you are engaged in a conversation and your dog suddenly takes off after a cat or a squirrel. He is running away from you, but if you call out, STAND STAY, he should freeze. Then summon him, PRINCE, COME. To practice this necessary skill, tie the dog to a tree or, if your dog is small, stand on his line. Use a 20-foot lead. Now, have someone call the dog. As he gallops from your side, watch the line play out and just before he reaches the end of it, call out, PRINCE, STAND STAY. If he keeps running, the end of the line will give him a jolt. Repeat the exercise until he learns to stop and stand, then call him back to HEEL, praising him with GOOD PRINCE, GOOD DOG. Practice this, using a variety of distractions until your dog responds perfectly to the command.

Your dog must not be allowed to jump on people or to continue playing when you order him to stop. If you don't control him, your dog will control you. Friends will dislike your little beast and you may find yourself wanting to get rid of this big headache which you yourself created.

One way to teach a dog not to jump up on people is to meet his chest with your knee, commanding, NO. That may work. You should ask others to do this as well should your dog jump on them. You don't want a dog who is obedient for you but pesters everyone else.

Another method is to gently step on the dog's back toes when he jumps up and say, NO. The little dog will learn this immediately because they know instinctively to protect themselves from injury. The larger dog does not feel as threatened by this move.

Now that you have the dog coming to you when you call him back, command, PRINCE, SIT STAY, and walk away from him, your arm stretched out shoulder-high, your fingers extended. If he stays, walk away a few more feet, repeating, STAY. Pause, then call him to you, once again praising him, GOOD PRINCE, GOOD DOG. If he doesn't stay, keep saying, NO, gently positioning him where you want him to be. If your dog continues to disobey, reposition him somewhat more forcefully until he stays. When he does stay, move away maybe two feet, then command STAY. Go two more feet, STAY. When you call him back to you, pet him to show your pleasure and praise him. This command may be a hard one for your dog to learn, but repeat it until he does. CAUTION. After trying this a few times, stop and play with him. Again, five minutes is time enough for one session. It is better to repeat the exercise four or five times with rest and play intervals, than to have your dog tire out or become discouraged.

Smoky learned the obedience trials, off the leash, in two days. The secret was to hold five-minute sessions and repeat them throughout the day. She learned to sit up, play dead dog and sing during these first sessions. Of course, she was exceptional.

The important thing about these early sessions is that your partner is learning your language. Later, hand signals may be all that your dog requires to obey. After you hold the dog away from you with your arm extended, give him the come motion by drawing your arm in to your chest saying, PRINCE, COME. In a short time, the motions will be enough. Practice with your dog in the SIT STAY and DOWN STAY positions, walking away facing him or with your back to him. Have others walk around him, too, so that he learns to STAY under any conditions.

After the dog comes when called, Obedience Trial routines require that the dog stop in front of you and then SIT. The next command is HEEL AROUND, at which the dog either walks to your right side and behind you to come to the heel position at your left knee and sits, or walks to his right just past you and turns to his left to take his place at the heel position and sits. After a few seconds, praise your dog as he tries to learn this. He will be sloppy at first, but your practice will make him perfect. Again, make those training sessions short with lots of play in between.

Animals, like people, must learn to obey in any circumstance and under all conditions. The roaring crowd, the blaring band and the children running underfoot are all distractions that can disrupt discipline. Athletes must compete in different arenas. Actors must be able to play as well to an audience as they do in rehearsals. Nothing must be allowed to interfere with a performance. Your dog must learn to concentrate on his disciplined behavior in any situation in order to be acceptable in society. Try to familiarize them with these various types of interruptions.

When your dog seems well-mannered enough, take him for walks around the block, testing him. Teach him to sit automatically when you stop, to heel automatically when you begin walking. At shopping centers, make him heel and behave when people stop to pet him or talk to him. This will be a new experience for him, and he must learn to obey. Watch how he reacts to children when they approach him. If he shows any apprehension, have him sit quietly. Some dogs have been treated roughly by children in the past and it may be wise to avoid them unless the dog has shown genuine affection for children beforehand.

TRICKS

You may want to teach your dog a few simple tricks like sitting up or begging. Here little treats can speed up the process. If your dog is not going to perform professionally, an occasional treat is all right.

Show your dog a biscuit and let him smell it. Have him sit still in front of you and say, NO, if he tries to grab the treat as you hold it over his nose. (Get down on your knees with a small dog.) Get him to rise on his haunches as he reaches for the treat. Say, SIT UP, and give him the biscuit if he does anything that even resembles sitting up, then let him hear and see how happy you are.

Try it again. Make him sit in front of you and wait, then make him sit for the treat, waiting longer each time before you give it to him. Practice this every night before bed and soon the two of you will have perfected his SIT UP.

Next, you may want to teach him to WALK on his hind legs. Some breeds are especially good at this. Fox Terriers, Poodles, Dalmatians and other agile, quick-moving dogs will do well. Heavy dogs like St. Bernards will have a hard time mastering it. Try to stay in the range of tricks easiest for your dog.

After your dog has mastered the SIT UP for his treat, hold the treat high over his head until he stretches up on his hind legs to get it. Keep it high enough and back far enough so that he has to walk around to keep it in sight. Say, WALK, as you keep it out of his reach. If he prances around a couple of steps, give it to him and say, GOOD PRINCE, GOOD DOG, accompanied by a lot of petting. Praise and petting must always follow his response to your commands. Try it again, making sure that he walks on his hind legs and doesn't jump. Only then does he get the biscuit. Once again, practice will produce a polished performance.

STRETCHING AND YAWNING

All dogs do some things naturally. Motion picture trainers learn to capitalize on this behavior. As a dog wakens, he usually stretches with his front paws forward and his back high. Then he stretches with his back legs out and his chest high. Next comes a big yawn. The trainer waits for the dog to waken, then as the dog begins the first stretch, the trainer calls, FRONT LEG STRETCH. Next, when the dog stretches the other way, the trainer calls, BACK LEG STRETCH. Finally, with the yawn, the trainer calls, BIG YAWN, and gives his pupil a treat.

Of course, the first time the trainer tries this, the dog thinks he is nuts. But, after a while, the dog will enjoy the exercise and the treats and will eventually do all these things on command.

GRAPEVINE

You may want your dog to learn to walk in and out through your legs, on the command, THROUGH THE LEGS. This is called the Grapevine. As you lead slowly with your right leg, with the dog on your left, pass the leash through your legs from left to right, gently leading the dog through to the outside of your right leg. Then, lead with your left leg, passing the leash from right hand to left. Do this back and forth a number of times, gently leading your dog through the paces. With lots of praise and practice, it won't be long before you are both able to synchronize this routine for as long as you desire to continue walking.

There are many tricks you can teach your pet. Invent some. Remember that he wants to please you by responding to your commands. Work with him. And always remember, PATIENCE, PATIENCE, PATIENCE AND PRAISE.

THE YORKSHIRE TERRIER

This has to be one of the greatest of the breeds. The Yorkshire Terrier as a breed is about 150 years old. The founding sire is thought to have been Huddersfield Ben. It is said that weavers from Scotland brought them to Yorkshire, England and used the larger dogs as ratters in the mines. Both short-haired and long-haired dogs are part of their background. The Yorkshire history contains a progression of the crossing of breeds, and some breeds that stamped many characteristics on the Yorkies no longer exist.

Pups are born mostly black and bear a resemblance to the Doberman. They have shiny, short hair and brown markings on the ears, face and lower legs. In a few months, their color changes to tan on their heads and legs. The body lightens from black to a dark hue or a lighter steel blue. In recent years a darker hue has been more in vogue. At a show I attended in 1994 I was told some judges now prefer the more light silver-blue. Their tails are docked. A breeder can tell in a 10-week-old how good the hair texture, markings and physical makeup will be in the adult dog. The best typy specimens go for the highest prices. The pet specimens sell for considerably less, although they have good genes.

The book, *The New Complete Yorkshire* (by Joan B. Gordon, Howell Pub., 1993), is the most definitive study of the history of the breed I have read. Joan and her late sister Janet Bennett, finished almost 300 American champion Yorkshire Terriers from their Wildweir Kennel. Anyone seriously considering raising and showing Yorkies will find this book indispensable.

Although they can range in size from one to seven pounds, most Yorkies weigh three to five pounds. Currently many dogs being shown and winning are in the 7 lb. range which is really a regression from the breed development to the toy size. Perhaps it is because the heavy demand for Yorkies makes more available at higher prices. Smaller specimens of good types have always brought higher prices. Some veteran breeders believe the showing of 7 lb. dogs is a fad. On that note does it mean eventually there may be 20 lb. and later 80 lb. yorkies in the future? Lets hope not! Poodles for example range from toys, miniatures and standards (large).

Size, intelligence, hardiness, gameness, friendliness, non-shedding hair and portability are among yorkie fine qualities.

The biggest disadvantage for the Yorkie is probably its size. The tiny dog does not have a high tolerance for manhandling by little children. It must be watched carefully if large dogs are anywhere near, but this is true of all small dogs. A larger dog could kill a Yorkie in an instant. Dogs are territorial and often attack canine intruders. A porky Yorkie can provoke a larger dog into a fight that might have fatal consequences. They are game little critters and outstanding mousers.

Their hair must be combed and brushed daily or snarls will make it necessary to cut it. Someone will have to bathe the Yorkie more often as part of its grooming. In former years, show dogs had hair, mustaches and sideburns as long as 17 inches after five years of growth. Now, the hair is kept cut to floor length for show.

We have not known them to have any eating problems. With proper diet and shots by a veterinarian, the Yorkie seems to fare well and has a long life expectancy. Generally, it is a hardy dog. Don't let your dog run free in winter, even in your own yard. Watch its feet in winter. In extremely cold weather, a small dog will have difficulty moving as its tiny foot pads quickly become chilled. This is especially true when rock salt is scattered on the ground. It makes the ice even colder and can hurt the large dog, too. If he starts to limp, take your dog immediately to a warm place. If you don't, he will become terribly uncomfortable, maybe even unable to move. Smoky was exposed to this hazard more often than the average dog because of all the traveling we did.

WHERE TO LOOK FOR A DOG. Remember that the serious fanciers of any breed make very little, if any, money on breeding. The costs run high for breeding stock, veterinarian bills, shots, medicines and food. Kennel maintenance, traveling expenses and handlers' fees drive up the cost per pup. Registering the dogs with the American Kennel Club and filing the dogs' papers add to the expense of breeding. A central agency can trace the lineage of your dog all the way back to the founding of the breed.

Beware of possible puppy factories in the shopping malls. Don't be taken in by a puppy's cuteness—all puppies are cute! Some of these pet shops rely on fly-by-night suppliers who are interested in the fast buck, not the quality and care of their animals. The dog's papers may not be legitimate, and often the dogs have not had any shots. The breeder may be legitimate, but the pet store may have bought left-overs, dogs that did not meet the breeder's standards. This practice is not condoned by the specialty clubs.

Other suppliers breed animals in their own factories, often under substandard and inhumane conditions. Some of these dealers have been so terrible that they have been the subjects of television exposes. Some pet sellers get high prices from laboratories. Stay away from these types and get your dog from a reliable breeder.

In many cities, breed clubs can be a source of information. Go to dog shows when they come around. There, you can meet the breeders, who will gladly talk with you about their specialty. You will find that these shows are usually advertised in advance.

When I brought Smoky home in 1945, she was the first Yorkie since 1937 to be shown in the Cleveland Classic, Western Reserve Kennel Club's largest show. Now, because the Yorkshire Terrier is among the most popular breeds, you will find them being shown everywhere.

Dog lovers' magazines, such as "Dog World," carry stories and pictures, as well addresses of specialty clubs and advertising about all breeds and kennels. These are published monthly and available at most magazine stands. "The Yorkshire Terrier" is an example of a breed magazine. Most breeds have specialty clubs. I am a founding member of the Yorkshire Terrier Club of America.

I have recently renewed my membership. This move brought latest information of the club's beginning of the new Yorkshire Terrier Club of America Foundation Inc. The YTCAF was started in February 1991 because the popularity of the breed has brought some rare diseases into prominence. This was done, because of inbreeding and when problems cropped up, some breeders continued to show and breed dogs with the defective genes instead of changing the breeding program. The same thing happened with quarter horses. Perfectly healthy looking horses began dropping into faints after exercising. It was recently traced to a very popular new-look type of handsome muscular stud, and the whole quarter horse breeding program is being investigated.

In Yorkies and with several other breeds, Portosystemic Shunt (liver shunt) is serious enough for the YTCA Foundation Inc. to start research on the problem headed by Dr. Larry Snyder DVM in conjunction with Michigan State University. Dr. Snyder also breeds Yorkies. This liver disease is caused by a recessive gene that has been brought forward by breeding practices.

There are other genetic/congenital diseases too and like other popular breeds, the public demand causes new people to enter into breeding, some of whom have not the interest of the breed in mind.

That is why contacting local or the national Yorkshire Terrier Club for the names of dependable kennels is important. This is true for any breed. DOG WORLD MAGAZINE publishes the current address of the Yorkshire Terrier Club of America as addresses change with election of new Presidents.

If you have the space, desire and the time to introduce a Yorkie into your household, doing some homework first will minimize troubles later. Overall, it is a delightful little dog that manages well in a big house or in a small apartment. Good luck!